THE BALCONY

THE BALCONY

JEAN GENET

Translated by
Barbara Wright and
Terry Hands

ff

faber and faber

LONDON · BOSTON

First published in 1958 by Faber and Faber Limited
in the translation by Bernard Frechtman
This translation by Barbara Wright and Terry Hands
first published in 1991 by
Faber and Faber Limited
3 Queen Square London WC1N 3AU

Photoset by Parker Typesetting Service Leicester

Printed in England by Clays Ltd St Ives plc

Barbara Wright and Terry Hands are hereby identified
as translators of this work, in accordance with Section 77
of the Copyright, Designs and Patents Act 1988

CIP data for this book is available
from the British Library

ISBN 0–571–15246–5

CONTENTS

PUBLISHER'S NOTE

This version of *The Balcony*, originally performed by the Royal Shakespeare Company in 1971, incorporates some scenes and other elements from the 1956 and 1960 texts which do not appear in the French text published in 1962.

The world première of *The Balcony* took place in April 1957 at the Arts Theatre Club, London. It was not performed in France until three years later, in May 1960, when Peter Brook directed it at the Théâtre du Gymnase, Paris. It was seen in New York in March 1960. The text used on all these occasions was a revised version.

The first production of this version, based on the original play, was performed at the Aldwych Theatre on 25 November 1971, with the following cast:

BISHOP	T. P. McKenna
IRMA (QUEEN)	Brenda Bruce
BISHOP'S GIRL (ROSINE)	Frances de la Tour
THIEF (MARLYSE)	Mary Rutherford
JUDGE	Clement McCallin
TORTURER (ARTHUR)	Hugh Keays Byrne
GENERAL	Philip Locke
GENERAL'S GIRL (ELYANE)	Helen Mirren
BEGGAR/SLAVE	Reg Lye
BEGGAR'S GIRL	Laura Graham
BLOOD (1ST PHOTOGRAPHER)	John York
TEARS (2ND PHOTOGRAPHER)	Ronald Forfar
SPERM (3RD PHOTOGRAPHER)	Ralph Cotterill
CARMEN	Estelle Kohler
CHIEF OF POLICE (GEORGE)	Barry Stanton
GEORGETTE	Holly Wilson
CHANTAL	Heather Canning
WOUNDED MAN	Colin Edwynn
ROGER	Patrick Stewart
ARMAND	Boyd Mackenzie
LOUIS	Patrick Godfrey
LUKE	Terence Taplin
MARK	John Wood
ENVOY	Alan Howard

MUSICIANS	Gordon Kember *or*
	Robert Stewart
	Tony McVey
	Robin Weatherall
Director	Terry Hands
Designer	Farrah
Music	Guy Woolfenden
Lighting	Steward Leviton

It was revived on 9 July 1987 at the Barbican Theatre, when the cast was as follows:

BISHOP	Richard Moore
IRMA (QUEEN)	Dilys Laye
BISHOP'S GIRL (ROSINE)	Valerie Buchanan
THIEF (MARLYSE)	Vivienne Rochester
JUDGE	Jim Carter
TORTURER (ARTHUR)	Howard Ward
GENERAL	Robert Demeger
GENERAL'S GIRL (ELYANE)	Cornelia Hayes
BEGGAR/SLAVE	Stuart Richman
BEGGAR'S GIRL	Pia Anderson
BLOOD (1ST PHOTOGRAPHER)	Malcolm Hassell
TEARS (2ND PHOTOGRAPHER)	Roger Moss
SPERM (3RD PHOTOGRAPHER)	Mark Lindley
CARMEN	Kathryn Pogson
CHIEF OF POLICE	Joe Melia
GEORGETTE	Penny Ryder
CHANTAL	Francesca Folan
WOUNDED MAN	Simon Cook
ROGER	Gerard Murphy
ARMAND	Trevor Gordon
LOUIS	Stan Petty
LUKE	Sidney Cole
MARK	Tom Knight
ENVOY	Richard Easton
Director	Terry Hands
Designer	Farrah
Music	Guy Woolfenden
Lighting	Terry Hands with Clive Morris

JEAN GENET
HOW TO PERFORM *The Balcony* (1962)

In London, at the Arts Theatre, I saw for myself that *The Balcony* was badly acted. It was equally badly acted in New York, Berlin and Paris – so I was told. In London, the director's sole aim was to abuse the English royal family, the Queen in particular, and to turn the scene between the General and his horse into a satire on war, with a decor of barbed wire.

Barbed wire in de luxe brothel!

In New York, the director quite simply cut everything to do with the revolution.

Berlin: the first director, a kind of Prussian corporal, had had the idea of transforming the apparatus that enables Madam Irma to see and hear everything that goes on in each of her salons into a kind of colour television set, in which the audience would have seen everything she described. He had another – Teutonic – idea: 1900 costumes for everyone.

Paris: the General was an admiral or a member of the Institute. Madam Irma – the actress playing the part, I mean – refused to be on stage at curtain rise and demanded that Carmen should speak the lines in the first scenes. The actresses changed the words, and the director cut the text.

In Vienna, in Basle, I've forgotten – or I never knew.

The revolving stage – Paris – was absurd: I want the scenes to follow one another, the sets to shift from left to right as if they were going to stack themselves up on top of each other under the eyes of the spectator. My intention is clear, though.

In the first four scenes almost everything should be played in an exaggerated fashion, although there are some passages in which the tone should be more natural, thus making the exaggeration seem more outrageous. In short, no equivocation, but two opposing tones.

On the other hand, from the scene between Madam Irma and Carmen until the end, the thing is to discover a narrative tone that is *always* equivocal, always shifting.

Are the feelings inspired in the protagonists by the situation real or false? Is the anger shown by the Chief of Police at the

Three Figures towards the end of the play real or false? Do the rebels exist *inside* the brothel or outside it? The equivocation must be maintained until the end.

The author of the play – particularly in so far as the last scene is concerned – would quite like it if no explanation is either cut or abridged under the pretext of getting through it more quickly, or of making things clearer, or that everything has already been said earlier, or that the audience has got the point, or is bored.

The actresses must not replace words like brothel, whorehouse, knocking-shop, cock, with polite words. They can refuse to act in my play – their place can be taken by men. Otherwise, they must respect what I have written. Although I don't mind if they say the words back to front – othelbray, for instance.

They must try to show signs of the rivalry that seems to exist between Irma and Carmen. I mean: who is the director (both of the house and of the play)? Carmen or Irma?

I had the idea of mounting the fundamental Three Figures on tall buskins. How can the actors walk on them without falling flat on their faces, catching their feet in the trains and laces of their skirts? They'll just have to learn.

It goes without saying that Irma's costume at the beginning of the play must be very austere. She may even seem to be in mourning. Not until the scene with Carmen does she doll herself up and wear the long dress that in the Balcony scene, with the help of a few decorations, becomes the Queen's dress.

As opposed to what was done in Paris, the Three Figures (Bishop, Judge, General) should be dressed in the uniforms or clothes current in the country where the play is being performed. What was wanted in France was a judge who resembled those in our assize courts, not a bewigged judge; the General needed a star-studded kepi or one encircled by oak leaves; he should not look like some kind of lord admiral. The costumes may be excessive, but should not be unrecognizable.

One shouldn't criticize all the time. In London, the director did have an idea: during one of the General's tirades, the actress playing the horse lovingly drew his moustaches on him with a bit of charcoal.

The photographers (last scene) must wear the outfits and adopt the mannerisms of the trendiest young people of the time and country in which the play is being performed. In France, in 1960, they had to be 'teddy-boys', in black leather and blue jeans.

The revolutionary type must be invented, and then painted on or modelled into a mask, for I cannot imagine anyone, even a protestant from Lyon, whose face would be long enough, sad enough and savage enough to play this part. The rigidity of masks would be quite suitable. But nothing in this scene must be cut.

The brief moments when Irma and the Chief of Police are alone together must reveal a long-standing affection. I don't know why.

Everything I have just written is not, of course, aimed at the intelligent director. He knows what to do. But what about the others?

One more thing: the play should not be performed as if it was a satire on this or that. It is – and must therefore be performed as – the glorification of the Image and the Reflection. Only then will its meaning – whether satirical or not – become apparent.

The imaginary representation of an action or an experience usually relieves us of the obligation of attempting to perform or undergo them ourselves, and in reality.

'When the problem of a certain disorder – or evil – has been solved on stage, this shows that it has in fact been abolished, since, according to the dramatic conventions of our times, a theatrical representation can only be the representation of a fact. We can then turn our minds to something else, and allow our hearts to swell with pride, seeing that we took the side of the hero who aimed – successfully – at finding the solution.'

This is what a conciliatory conscience is always suggesting to the audience. However, no problem that has been exposed ought to be solved in the imagination, especially when the dramatist has made every effort to show the concrete reality of a social order. On the contrary, the evil shown on stage should explode, should show us naked, and leave us distraught, if possible, and having no other recourse than ourselves.

It is not the function of the artist or the poet to find a practical solution to the problems of evil. They must resign themselves to being accursed. They may thereby lose their soul, if they have one; that doesn't matter. But the work must be an active explosion, an act to which the public reacts – as it wishes, as it can. If the 'good' is to appear in a work of art it does so through the divine aid of the powers of song, whose strength alone is enough to magnify the evil that has been exposed.

A few poets, these days, go in for a very curious operation: they sing the praises of the People, of Liberty, of the Revolution, etc., which, when sung, are rocketed up into an abstract sky and then stuck there, discomfited and deflated, to figure in deformed constellations. Disembodied, they become untouchable. How can we approach them, love them, live them, if they are dispatched so magnificently far away? When written – sometimes sumptuously – they become the constituent signs of a poem, and as poetry is nostalgia and the song destroys its pretext, our poets destroy what they wanted to bring to life.

Maybe I'm not making myself clear?

In the ceiling, a chandelier which remains the same in every scene.

The decor appears to represent a sacristy, formed by three blood-red satin screens.

In the screen at the back, a door.

Above it, an enormous trompe-l'œil *Spanish crucifix.*

On the right-hand partition, a mirror in a carved and gilded frame reflects an unmade bed which, if the room were logically arranged, would be in the auditorium, in the front row of the stalls.

A table with a water jug.

A yellow armchair.

On the armchair, a pair of black trousers, a shirt, a jacket.

The BISHOP, *mitred and wearing a golden cope, is sitting in the armchair. He is obviously more than life-sized. The part is played by an actor mounted on tragedians' buskins about 50 cm tall. His shoulders, with the cope over them, have been vastly broadened, so that at curtain rise he looks like a scarecrow, rigid and out of proportion. His face is exaggeratedly made up.*

By his side, a heavily made-up youngish woman in a lace negligée is drying her hands on a towel.

Standing, a dark-haired woman of about forty with a stern face, dressed in a severe black costume. This is IRMA. *She is wearing a hat. A hat with a string pulled tight like a chin strap.*

BISHOP: (*Sitting in the chair, in the centre of the stage, in a low but ardent voice*) Verily, that which distinguishes the prelate is not so much meekness – nor mildness – but a most rigorous intelligence. The heart is our undoing. We believe ourselves the master of our own beneficence – we know ourselves the slave of a serene flaccidity. Perhaps our distinction is something more than intelligence. (*Hesitates.*) It could be cruelty. And over and above this cruelty – therefrom – thereby – an advance – callid, virile – Towards Absence. Towards Death. And where does God figure in all this? (*Smiles.*) I knew you'd ask me that. (*To his mitre*) O mitre! Episcopal mitre! Bishop's archèd crown! Remember – that when my eyes close for the last time, it is you that I shall see within their lids, you my beautiful gilded hat, you my beautiful vestments, my copes, my lace . . .

IRMA: (*Ruthlessly*) That'll be twenty quid!
(*During the whole of this scene* IRMA *hardly moves. She is standing very near the door.*)

BISHOP: (*Very gently waves her aside*) Ssh!

IRMA: Twenty quid, and stop pissing about, or I'll start. And you know what that means . . . Now, if there's anything else I can do for you.

BISHOP: (*Dryly, tossing the mitre aside*) Thanks a lot.

IRMA: Steady with the props! That's got to last! (*To the* GIRL) Put it away.
(*She puts the mitre on the table, near the jug.*)

BISHOP: (*After a heavy sigh*) They say that this place is going to be surrounded. The rebels have already crossed the river.

IRMA: (*Worried*) There's blood everywhere . . . I should keep to the wall past the Archbishop's palace, if I were you. And then go through the fish market.
(*A sudden scream of pain from a woman offstage.*)
(*Irritated*) I told them to keep quiet. Thank God I had the window padded. (*Suddenly friendly and insidious*) And what did we manage this evening? A benediction? A prayer? A Mass? A perpetual adoration?

GIRL: There was a benediction, Madam. And then my confession . . .

IRMA: Then what?

BISHOP: That's enough! Don't tell her!

GIRL: That's all. Except for my absolution.

IRMA: That's all! Then why can't anyone watch? Hm? Just once?

BISHOP: (*Terrified*) Oh no. Such things must – and shall remain secret. It's indecent even to talk about them while I'm being undressed. No one must watch – ever! And all the doors must be shut. Properly shut, closed, buttoned, laced, hooked, sewn . . .

IRMA: I was only asking . . .

BISHOP: Sewn *up*, Madam. Anyway, I don't wish to talk about it. *Consummatum est.* Hello! I'm speaking Latin! All I'm worried about now is my getting home.

IRMA: And all I'm worried about now is my twenty quid.

BISHOP: (*His voice becomes clearer and more precise, as if he had just woken up. He betrays a certain amount of irritation*) We didn't exactly strain ourselves, you know. Only six sins, and far from my favourite ones.

GIRL: What do you mean, only six! They were deadly ones. And I had a hell of a job finding those.

BISHOP: (*Worried*) You mean they weren't real?

GIRL: Of course they were real! What I mean is: I had a job committing them. If you only knew how difficult disobedience is – what you have to go through . . .

BISHOP: I can imagine, my child, I can imagine. The permissive society has reached a point where it is almost impossible to find anything that is *not* permitted . . . But if your sins were not real, now is the time to say so.

IRMA: Oh no it isn't. I can just hear you rabbiting on about it the next time you come. No. They were real, all right. (*To the* GIRL) Undo his laces. Take off his shoes. But don't let him catch cold. (*To the* BISHOP) D'you want a hot drink? What about a toddy?

BISHOP: No thanks. I haven't got the time. I must go. (*Dreamily*) Yes, six, but deadly ones!

IRMA: Come here. You've got to get undressed.

BISHOP: (*Pleading, almost on his knees*) Oh no, not yet.

IRMA: Time's up. Come on! Quick! Hurry up!
(*As she speaks, they undress him. Or, rather they undo some pins, and untie some bits of cord which look as if they are fastenings of his cope, his stole and his surplice.*)

BISHOP: (*To the* GIRL) Those sins – you really did commit them, didn't you?

GIRL: Yes.

BISHOP: And the things you did – you really meant them, didn't you? All of them?

GIRL: Yes.

BISHOP: And when you came towards me with your face uplifted, it really was transfigured by fire, wasn't it?

GIRL: Yes.

BISHOP: And when my forgiving hand descended, heavy with its rings, upon your forehead . . .

GIRL: Yes.

3

BISHOP: And when I looked deep into your lovely eyes?

GIRL: Yes.

IRMA: You saw repentance in those lovely eyes, didn't you, my Lord Bishop . . .

GIRL: Yes.

IRMA: You saw repentance.

BISHOP: (*Standing up*) Just about. But was it repentance I was looking for? What I *saw* was an insatiable longing for sin. She was submerged in evil – baptized by it! Her great eyes widened on to the abyss – the pallor of death gave life – yes, Madam Irma – *life*, to her face. And all our sanctity was created for that very reason, that we might forgive her those very sins. Even if they were phoney.

GIRL: (*Suddenly flirtatious*) And what if my sins were real?

BISHOP: (*in a different, less theatrical, tone of voice*) You must be out of your mind! You didn't really do all that, I hope?

IRMA: Don't be silly! Both of you! You needn't worry about her sins. There's no possibility . . .

BISHOP: I know . . . I know: There's no possibility of doing evil here. Because you live in evil. In the absence of remorse. And if you live in evil, you can't do evil. Right? The devil's a play-actor too. That's how you recognize him. He's the great actor. Which is why the Church has always anathametized the profession.

GIRL: Reality frightens you, doesn't it?

BISHOP: Look – if they were real, your sins would be crimes, and I'd be in the shit.

GIRL: Would you go to the police?

(IRMA *goes on undressing him. But he still has the cope over his shoulders.*

The same terrible scream is heard again.)

IRMA: They're at it again! I'll have to go and shut them up.

BISHOP: That was a real scream.

IRMA: (*Worried*) Was it? Oh, I don't know . . . How can we ever know? Anyway, what does it matter?

BISHOP: (*Slowly going up to the mirror, and then standing in front of it*) . . . Mirror, mirror, on the wall . . . Why do I come here? To find evil? To find innocence? (*To* IRMA, *very gently*) Go away! Leave me alone!

4

IRMA: It's late. It's getting more and more dangerous.

BISHOP: (*Pleading*) Just one more minute.

IRMA: You've already been here two hours and twenty minutes. That's twenty 'one-more-minutes' over your time.

BISHOP: (*Suddenly furious*) Leave me alone. Listen at the door if you want to – I know you do, anyway – and don't come back till I've finished.

(*The two women sigh and go out, looking as if they can't take any more.*

(*The* BISHOP *is left alone. He makes a visible effort to recover his composure, and then standing in front of the mirror, holding his surplice.*)

Now answer me, mirror, answer me. *Do* I come here to find innocence and evil? In your gilded glass, what am I? Here, in the sight of God, I swear – I have never, never aspired to the episcopal throne. To become a bishop, to rise in the hierarchy – whether by virtue or vice – would have meant my becoming further and further removed from the ultimate dignity of being a bishop. Let me explain: (*Now speaks in an extremely precise tone of voice, as if he were developing a logical argument*) if I had wanted to become a bishop, I should have had to put all my energy not into being one, but into acting in the sort of way that would have led to my becoming one. And if I had become a bishop for the sake of being one – for the sake of being one for my own sake, of course – I should have always had to remember my being one, in order fully to fulfil my function. Have I made myself clear?

(*He suddenly grabs hold of the flap of his surplice and kisses it.*)
O lace, lace, worked by a thousand tiny hands to veil all those heavenly breasts, those bulging breasts, and faces, and hair, you ennoble me with your effoliant veins and whirls. But where was I? – Ah yes, and here's the crux. Hello! There I go again! . . . – a function is only a function. It isn't a mode of being. But a bishop – that *is* a mode of being. It's a heavy responsibility. A burden. Mitres, lace, cloth of gold, costume jewellery . . . Stuff functions!

(*A burst of machine-gun fire.*)

IRMA: (*Putting her head through the half-open door*) Have you finished?

BISHOP: Oh for Christ's sake, leave me alone. Fuck off! I'm searching my soul.

(IRMA *shuts the door*.)

The majesty, the dignity, that illumine my person, do not emanate from my function – nor from my personal merits, by heaven! – the majesty, and dignity, that illumine me, irradiate from a more mysterious source: from the Bishop in me taking precedence over me. Have I made myself clear, mirror? Golden image! Ornate as a Mexican cigar box – and I want to *be* Bishop in solitude, in appearance only . . . And in order to destroy every vestige of function, I'm going to create a scandal – I'm going to violate you, you slut, you punk, you strumpet, you cunt!

IRMA: (*Coming back*) That does it. You've got to go.

BISHOP: Don't be ridiculous. I haven't finished.

(*Both women have come back*.)

IRMA: Look, I'm not quarrelling just for the fun of it. I'm telling you, you've no time to lose . . .

BISHOP: (*Ironically*) What you mean is, you need the room for someone else, and you've got to arrange the mirrors and jugs.

IRMA: (*Very irritated*) That's no business of yours. I've given you every attention while you've been here. I'm telling you, it's dangerous to hang about in the streets, whoever you are.

(*The sound of gun-fire in the distance*.)

BISHOP: (*Bitterly*) You don't give a fuck for my safety. When our time's up, you don't give a fuck for any of us!

IRMA: (*To the* GIRL) Undress him.

(*To the* BISHOP, *who has come down from his buskins and is now the size of a normal actor – the size of the most ordinary of actors*) Come on – help. You've gone all stiff.

BISHOP: (*Looking vacuous*) Stiff? I've gone stiff. Ritual stiffness! Final immobility . . .

IRMA: (*To the* GIRL) Give him his jacket.

BISHOP: (*Looking at his gear piling up on the floor*) My vestments, my lace – through you I re-enter myself. I reconquer a whole domain. I lay siege to an ancient fortress, from which I was once expelled. I take up my abode in a glade where at last suicide is possible. The decision rests with me, and here I stand face to face with my own death.

IRMA: Very beautiful – but you've got to go. You left your car by
the side door – near the pylon.
BISHOP: (*To* IRMA) Because our poor incompetent Chief of Police
can't stop the mob cutting our throats!
(*Turning back to the mirror and declaiming*) Vestments! Mitres!
Lace! Above all, my gilded cope – *you* protect me from the
world. Where are my legs, where are my arms? Under your
lustrous watered silk, what are my hands doing? They are
incapable of anything but the vaguest of fluttering gestures,
they've become truncated wings – not angels' wings, guinea-
fowls' wings – O rigid cope – you provide the warmth and
darkness for the most loving, the most luminous tenderness
to ripen. My loving kindness, which is destined to inundate
the world – it was distilled under your carapace. Did my
hand sometimes, like a knife, emerge to give benediction? Or
to slice, to scythe? My hand, a tortoise head, would separate
the two sides of my garment. Tortoise, or cautious adder?
Would go back into its rock. My hand, underneath, in its
retreat, would dream . . . Vestments, gilded copes . . .
(*The stage moves from left to right, as if it were being swallowed
up by the wings. The next set then appears.*)

SCENE 2

*Same chandelier. Three brown screens. Bare walls. On the right, the
same mirror, reflecting the same unmade bed as in the first scene.*

*A beautiful young woman looks as if she's in chains, with her wrists
bound. Her muslin dress is torn. Her breasts are visible.*

The TORTURER *is standing in front of her. He is a giant, and is
stripped to the waist. Bulging with muscles. His belt buckles at the
back: his whip is stuck behind the buckle, so that it looks as if he has a
tail.*

A JUDGE. *When he stands up he looks enormous, because he too is
mounted on buskins, which are invisible under his robe. His face is
exaggeratedly made up. At the moment he is crawling up to the woman
on his stomach. As he gets nearer to her she retreats step by step.*
THIEF: (*Extending her foot to him*) Not yet! Lick it! Lick it first . . .
(*The* JUDGE *makes an effort to go on crawling, then gets up and,*

7

slowly and painfully, though he looks happy, goes and sits down on a stool. The THIEF (*the lady described above*) *drops her domineering attitude and becomes humble.*)

JUDGE: (*Severely*) You are a thief! They caught you . . . The police caught you . . . You had forgotten that, whatever you did and wherever you did it, you could never escape the impenetrable filigree of my steely police. They're like swivel-eyed insects, my police, they're always watching you – watching you all! And they'll catch you all and bring you all to judgement. How do you plead? You were caught . . . under your skirt . . . (*To the* TORTURER) Put your hand under her skirt . . . you'll find her secret sporran, the celebrated Kangaroo pouch. (*To the* THIEF) Which you stuff with your haphazard loot. Because you're insatiable, indiscriminate, and injudicious . . . What's more, you're a bloody half-wit. (*To the* TORTURER) What did you find in that famous Kangaroo pouch? In that colossal paunch?

TORTURER: Perfumes, my Lord, one flash-light, one fly-squirt, two oranges, five pairs of socks, one large sea-urchin, one bathtowel and a red sash. (*To the* JUDGE) You're not listening. I said: a red sash

JUDGE: (*With a start*) A red sash? Ah, ah, yes – a red sash! We've got there already. Right! What, may I ask, were you going to do with a red sash – *the* red sash? Hm? – What were you going to do with it? Who were you going to strangle? Answer me. To strangle . . . hm? Who? Are you a thief or a strangler? (*Very softly, appealing to her*) Tell me, my child, tell me, I implore you, tell me you're a thief.

THIEF: OK, my Lord.

TORTURER: No!

THIEF: (*Looking at him in amazement*) No?

TORTURER: That comes later.

THIEF: What?

TORTURER: I said: your confession comes later. Deny it.

THIEF: But I'll get hit again!

JUDGE: (*In honeyed tones*) Precisely, my child: you'll get hit. You have to deny it first, then admit it, and then repent. From forth your lovely eyes, I await the gush of warm springs. Oh! the power of tears! I want to be drenched in them . . .

Where's my statute book? (*Puts his hand under his robes and brings out a book.*)

THIEF: But I've already cried . . .

JUDGE: (*Looking as if he's reading*) Because you were being hit. What I want is tears of repentance. I shan't be satisfied until you're as moist as a meadow.

THIEF: It's not very easy. I was trying to cry just now . . .

JUDGE: (*Has stopped reading. In a half-theatrical but almost casual tone of voice*) You're very young. Are you new here? (*Anxiously*)You're not under age, are you?

THIEF: Oh no, Sir . . .

JUDGE: Call me my Lord. How long have you been here?

TORTURER: Since the day before yesterday, my Lord.

JUDGE: (*Resuming both his theatrical tone of voice and his reading*) Let her speak. I like her voice. I like that sparse, puling, sound. Now listen: You've got to be a model thief, if you want me to be a model judge. Phoney thief, phoney judge. Got it!

THIEF: Oh yes, my Lord.

JUDGE: (*Still reading*) Good! So far, everything's gone swimmingly. My torturer has hit you very hard – because that's his job you see. We're inseparable: we three. Example: if he *didn't* hit you, how could I *stop* him hitting you? He *has* to hit you because I *have* to intervene to prove my authority. So you see: you *have* to deny everything, so that he *can* hit you. (*The sound of something falling in the next room. In a normal tone of voice*) What's that? Are all the doors properly shut? Can anyone see us, or hear us?

TORTURER: Of course not! Don't worry. I bolted the door. (*He goes and checks an enormous bolt on the rear door.*) And the corridor's out of bounds.

JUDGE: (*Speaking naturally*) Are you sure?

TORTURER: Positive. (*He puts his hand in his pocket.*) Can I have a fag?

JUDGE: (*Speaking naturally*) Go ahead. The smell of tobacco inspires me.

(*Same sound as before.*)

Oh, what on earth *is* that? What *is* it? When am I going to get some peace? (*Stands up*) What's going on?

TORTURER: (*Drily*) Nothing's going on. Someone must have dropped something. You're just nervy.

JUDGE: (*Speaking naturally, casually*) Maybe. But it pays to be nervy – stops me missing things!
(*He stands up and walks over to the wall.*)
Can I have a look?

TORTURER: Just a peep. It's getting late. (*Shrugs his shoulders and exchanges a wink with the* THIEF.)

JUDGE: (*After he has looked*) It's lit – brightly lit – but empty.

TORTURER: (*Shrugging his shoulders*) Empty!

JUDGE: (*Speaking even more casually than before*) You look worried. Is there any news?

TORTURER: This afternoon, just before you arrived, three key positions fell to the rebels. They started some fires, but not a single fireman turned out. The town's in flames. The High Court . . .

JUDGE: What about the Chief of Police? Doing sweet FA as usual, I suppose?

THIEF: We've not had any news of him for the last four hours. He's bound to come here, if he can get away at all. We're expecting him any minute now.

JUDGE: (*Sitting down, to the* THIEF) Anyway, he'd better not try and come over Queen's Bridge.

TORTURER: Why not?

JUDGE: It was blown up last night. (*Giggles.*)

THIEF: (*Exasperated*) We knew that. We heard the explosion from here.

JUDGE: (*Resuming his theatrical way of speaking, and reading from his statute book*) Right. Where were we? Taking advantage of the sleep of the just, then, taking advantage of a moment's sleep, you ransack and rob, you pilfer and pinch, you steal, you swipe, you snaffle, you snitch, you nick, you knock-off . . .

THIEF: No, my Lord, never . . .

TORTURER: Shall I let her have it?

THIEF: (*Shrieking*) Arthur!

TORTURER: What the hell's the matter with you? You mustn't speak to me! You must answer his Lordship. And don't call me Arthur. I'm the Torturer, remember?

THIEF: Yes, Mr Torturer.

JUDGE: (*Reading*) To resume: did you steal?

THIEF: Yes. Yes, my Lord.

JUDGE: (*Reading*) Good. And now answer quickly, and tell the truth, the whole truth, and nothing but the truth: what else did you steal?

THIEF: Some bread, my Lord – because I was hungry.

JUDGE: (*Drawing himself up to his full height and putting his book down*) Sublime! Sublime function! Perfumes, one flash light, one fly-squirt, two oranges, five pairs of socks, one large sea-urchin, one bath-towel, a red sash and *some* bread. I shall have all that to judge. Oh, my child, you reconcile me to the world. Judge! I am going to be the judge of your actions! The scales of justice hang balanced from my hands. The world is an apple: I cut it in two – good people and bad people. You do agree, don't you, you do agree to be one of the bad? Thank you very much –
(*Turning to face the audience*) Ladies and gentlemen, before your very eyes – with nothing up my sleeve, nothing in my hands – I separate the rottenness and throw it away. But this is a painful process. To pronounce every sentence with the gravity it deserves would cost me my life. Which is why I am dead. This is the region, that region of total freedom that I inhabit. King of the Infernal Regions, those I weigh in the balance are, like me, dead. That, like me, is one of the dead.

THIEF: I'm scared, Sir.

JUDGE: (*Grandiloquently*) Silence! In the furthest deeps of Hades, I separate the humans who venture there. Some I consign to the flames, others to the boredom of the Elysian fields. Listen you, thief – spy – bitch – it's Minos speaking to you. Minos is weighing you in the balance.
(*To the* TORTURER) Cerberus?

TORTURER: (*Imitating a dog*) Woof Woof!

JUDGE: Good dog! How beautiful you are. And how your beauty rises at the sight of another victim. (*He pulls back the* TORTURER's *lips*) Show your fangs! Terrible! White! (*He suddenly looks worried. To the* THIEF) You really did commit those thefts, didn't you? You're not lying, are you?

TORTURER: Of course she committed them, for Christ's sake!

She wouldn't have dared *not* commit them!

JUDGE: I am almost happy. Go on. What did you steal?

(*A sudden burst of machine-gun fire.*)

Oh, not again! Never a moment's peace.

THIEF: I told you: the fighting has spread all over the northern part of the town . . .

TORTURER: Wrap up!

JUDGE: (*Irritated*) Are you – or are you not – going to answer me? What else did you steal? Where? When? How? How much? Why? For whom? Answer me.

THIEF: I often used to sneak in to houses when the maids were out: I'd use the tradesmen's entrance, of course . . . I used to steal things out of drawers, I'd break open the children's piggy-banks. (*She is obviously having difficulty in finding her words.*) Once I dressed up to look respectable. I had on a puce-coloured suit, a black straw hat with cherries and a little veil, and black, low-heeled shoes . . . So, naturally, I got in . . .

JUDGE: (*Who can't wait to hear*) Where? Where? Where? Where? Where? Where? Where did you get in?

THIEF: I don't remember. I'm sorry.

TORTURER: Shall I let her have it?

JUDGE: Not yet. (To the THIEF) Where did you get in? Just tell me where.

THIEF: (*In a panic*) But I don't remember, I swear I don't.

TORTURER: Shall I hit her, my Lord? Shall I hit her?

JUDGE: (*To the* TORTURER, *walking towards him*) Ah! Ha! So you like beating, do you? You please me, Torturer! You great big mountain of meat, motivated only by my order. (*Pretends to be looking at himself in the Torturer.*) Mirror – in which I am glorified! Image I can touch – I love you. Never would I have had the strength or the skill to mark her with such fiery stripes. And, anyway, what would I want with all that strength and skill? (*Touches him*) You're there, aren't you? Yes, you are, my enormous arm – too heavy for me, too gross, much too gross for my shoulder, yet walking of your own accord at my side! Arm, vast shoulder of beef – I wouldn't exist without you . . . (*To the* THIEF) Nor without you, my child. You are my two perfect complements . . .

Don't we make a pretty trio! (*To the* THIEF) But *you* have the advantage over him and over me, because you came first. My existence as a judge is an emanation of your existence as a thief. You'd only have to refuse – but you'd better not . . .! to refuse to be who you are – what you are, and therefore who you are – for me to stop existing . . . for me to vanish, to evaporate. Exploded! Repudiated! Burst! Ergo: good springs from . . .? from . . .? But you won't refuse, will you? You won't refuse to be a thief? That would be evil. That would be criminal. You would be depriving me of my existence! (*Imploring her*) Tell me, my child, my love – you won't refuse, will you?

THIEF: (*Coyly*) Well . . . you never know . . .

JUDGE. What's that? What did you say? You *would* refuse? You! Tell me where, and tell me again, what you stole, this instant!

THIEF: Who do you think you're talking to? Do you mind!

JUDGE: My dear young lady . . . Madam. *Please*. (*Throws himself on to his knees.*) Look – I'm on my knees. Don't leave me like this, I beg of you – *waiting* to be a judge. If there weren't any judges, what would become of us? And, if there weren't any thieves . . .

THIEF: (*Ironically*) Then what?

JUDGE: It would be terrible. But you wouldn't do that to me, would you? You won't make it so that there aren't any? Please understand me: providing you don't ultimately refuse to confess, you can prevaricate as long as you like, or as long as my nerves will stand it – you can keep me on tenterhooks, make me fret, froth, sweat, rampage, crawl . . . would you like me to crawl?

TORTURER: (*To the* JUDGE) Yes!

JUDGE: I have my pride, you know!

TORTURER: (*Threateningly*) Crawl!

(*The* JUDGE, *who was on his knees, lies flat on his stomach and slowly crawls up to the* THIEF. *As he gets nearer to her, the* THIEF *retreats step by step.*)

Good. Keep going.

JUDGE: (*To the* THIEF) You're quite right to make me crawl for the privilege of being a judge, you slut, but if you finally denied me my existence, you cow, that would be criminal . . .

THIEF: (*Haughtily*) Call me Madam, and ask politely.

JUDGE: Will I get what I want?

THIEF: (*Coyly*) Expensive business, stealing.

JUDGE: I'll pay! I'll pay whatever it costs, Madam. But, if I couldn't separate Good and Evil any more, what on earth would be the use of me, I wonder?

THIEF: So do I.

JUDGE: (*Infinitely sad*) Just now, I was going to be Minos. My Cerberus was barking. (*To the* TORTURER) Do you remember?
(*The* TORTURER *interrupts the* JUDGE *by cracking his whip.*) You were so cruel, so vicious! (*Savouring the memory.*) Hm! And I was pitiless. I was going to fill the Infernal Regions with the damned. I was going to fill the prisons. All the prisons! Prisons! Prisons! Cells, blessed places where evil cannot exist, for they are the crossroads of all the world's malediction. Evil cannot be committed within evil. And what I desire above all things is not to condemn, but to judge . . . (*Tries to get up.*)

TORTURER: Keep crawling! And get a move on – I've got to go and get dressed.

JUDGE: (*To the* THIEF) Madam! Madam! – please say yes – I beg of you – please don't refuse. I'm ready to lick your shoes with my tongue – but say you're a thief . . .

THIEF: (*Shouting*) Not yet! Lick them! Lick them! Lick them first!
(*The stage moves from left to right, as it did at the end of the previous scene, and is swallowed up into the wings on the right. In the distance, a burst of machine-gun fire.*)

SCENE 3

Three screens, in the same position as in the preceding scenes, but dark green. The same chandelier. The same mirror, reflecting the unmade bed. On the armchair a horse, like those used by country dancers, with a little pleated skirt. There is a timid-looking man in the room. He is

14

the GENERAL. *He has taken off his jacket, then his bowler hat and gloves.* IRMA *is standing near him.*

GENERAL: (*Pointing to his hat, jacket and gloves*) Get rid of these things, will you?

IRMA: Certainly, I'll have them folded and wrapped in tissue.

GENERAL: I just don't want to see them any more.

IRMA: I'll have them put away – I might even have them burnt.

GENERAL: Oh, what a good idea! – I'd like them to be burnt. Like towns at dusk!

IRMA: Did you see anything on your way here?

GENERAL: I ran terrible risks. The people have been blowing up the dams, and whole districts are flooded. The arsenal's one of the worst-hit – the ammunition's got wet, and the guns have all gone rusty. I had to make quite a few big detours you know – but I didn't actually trip over any dead bodies.

IRMA: Well, I won't ask you what you think about all this. After all, it's a free country. Politics don't really interest me anyway.

GENERAL: Let's change the subject, then. What really interests me is how I'm going to get home. It'll be late by the time I'm finished.

IRMA: About being late.

GENERAL: Ah, yes. Sorry.
   (*He fumbles in his pocket, extracts some bank notes, counts them and gives some to* IRMA. *She keeps them in her hand.*)
   The point is I'm not wildly happy about getting picked off on my way home tonight. Obviously, there won't be anyone to see me home, will there?

IRMA: 'Fraid not. Unfortunately, Arthur's not free.
   (*A long silence.*)

GENERAL: (*Suddenly impatient*) What's the matter with her – isn't she coming?

IRMA: I've no idea what she's doing. I told them to have everything ready when you arrived. At least the horse is here . . . I'll ring.

GENERAL: No, no, I'll take charge of that. (*Rings.*) I like ringing. It's authoritative – ringing the charge!

IRMA: Not just yet, General . . . Oh, I'm sorry, there I go, giving you your rank already – Not yet, eh? – but any minute now –

GENERAL: Ssh! Don't say it.

IRMA: Ah! Such youth, such vigour, such panache!

GENERAL: And the spurs – I will have spurs, won't I? I did say I
wanted them fixed to my boots. Ox-blood boots. Right?

IRMA: Right, General. Ox-blood boots. And patent leather.

GENERAL: Patent leather, good, with mud on them?

IRMA: With mud, yes, and possibly a little blood. And then, of
course, there's the medals!

GENERAL: Authentic?

IRMA: Authentic!

(*Suddenly, a woman's long drawn-out scream.*)

GENERAL: What's that?

(*He goes over towards the wall on the right and is stooping to look
through it, but* IRMA *blocks his view.*)

IRMA: Nothing. Just a bit of involuntary improvisation.

GENERAL: But that scream. That was a woman's scream. A lady
is in distress. My heart missed a beat. I leap to the rescue.
Like a thunderbolt, I –

IRMA: (*Icily*) Cool it, General, cool it. You're still in civvies,
remember.

GENERAL: So I am.

(*Another female scream.*)

All the same, it is a bit upsetting, you know – inconvenient,
too.

IRMA: Where on earth is she?

(*She goes over to the bell, but a very beautiful young redhead
enters by the rear door, her dishevelled hair hanging loose. Her
bosom is almost bare. She is wearing only a black corset, black
stockings and very high-heeled shoes. She is carrying a full
general's uniform, complete with sword, cocked hat and boots.*)

GENERAL: (*Severely*) So there you are! Half an hour late. Battles
have been lost in less time than that.

IRMA: She'll make up for it, General. I know her.

GENERAL: (*Looking at the boots*) Where's the blood? I can't see the
blood.

IRMA: It's dried. Don't forget that it's the blood of your former
battles. Right. I'll leave you. Do you need anything else?

GENERAL: (*Looking to right and left*) You're forgetting . . .

IRMA: Good God! So I was.

(She puts down on to the chair the towels she had been carrying over her arm. Then she goes out, rear. The GENERAL *goes over to the door and locks it. But the moment the door is shut, there is a knock. The* GIRL *goes to open it. Standing some way behind it, sweating, and wiping himself with a towel, is the* TORTURER.)

TORTURER: Where's Madam Irma?

GIRL: *(Abruptly)* In the Rose Garden. *(Correcting herself)* Sorry: the Chapel of Rest. *(Shuts the door.)*

GENERAL: *(Irritated)* They'll leave me in peace now – I hope. And you're late — what on earth were you up to? Didn't you get your oats? You're smiling, aren't you? Smiling at your rider? Him? Do you recognize his hand – firm but gentle? *(He strokes her.)* My fiery steed! My beautiful mare – Ah, what lovely gallops we've had together!

GIRL: And there are more to come! With my well-shod hooves, and my quivering fetlocks, I shall tread the world . . . Take off your trousers and shoes, and let me dress you.

GENERAL: *(With the riding-whip in his hand)* Yes, yes, but first – on your knees! On your knees! Come on, come on, bend your hocks, bend . . .

(The GIRL *rears, whinnies with pleasure, and kneels in front of the* GENERAL *like a circus horse.)*

Bravo! Bravo, Dove! You haven't forgotten a thing. And now you must help me, and answer my questions. It's only natural for a well-bred filly to help her master undo himself, take his things off, and give him tit for tat. Right, start by undoing my laces.

(During the whole of the following scene, the GIRL *is helping the* GENERAL *to undress, and then to put on his general's uniform. When he is completely dressed, he will be seen to have assumed gigantic proportions, due to various theatrical devices: invisible buskins, padded shoulders, exaggerated make-up.)*

GIRL: Is your left foot still swollen?

GENERAL: Yes. It's my best foot. The one I put forward. Like your hoof when you toss your head.

GIRL: Now what do you want me to do? Go on – undo yourself.

GENERAL: Are you a horse or an illiterate? If you're a horse – toss your head. Help me. Pull. No, no – not so hard, you're not a cart-horse.

GIRL: I'm doing what I'm supposed to do.

GENERAL: What! Mutiny? Already? Just wait till I'm ready! Just wait till I put the bit between your teeth.

GIRL: Oh no, not that. Anything but that.

GENERAL: A general reprimanded by his horse! You'll get the full harness for this, the snaffle, the bit, the bridle, the girth and, booted and helmeted, I'll whip and plunge.

GIRL: The bit is terrible. It makes your lips bleed, and your gums. I'll be dribbling blood.

GENERAL: Pink froth in your mouth – celestial fire in your loins! What a gallop! through the rye-fields, into the clover, over the meadows and along the dusty roads, over hill and down dale, asleep or awake, from dawn to dusk, and from dusk –

GIRL: Tuck in your shirt. Pull up your braces. It's quite a job, dressing a victorious general – especially one we're going to bury. Do you want your sabre?

GENERAL: Leave it on the table, like Lafayette's. Where people will see it – but hide the clothes.

GIRL: Where?

GENERAL: I don't know – find somewhere!

(*The* GIRL *makes a neat pile of his clothes and hides them behind an armchair.*)

And the tunic? Good. Has it got all its medals? Count them!

GIRL: (*Counting very quickly*) All there!

GENERAL: And the war? Where's the war?

GIRL: (*Very gently*) It's coming, General – it's coming! It's evening in the orchard. The sky is calm and pink. A strange peace bathes the earth – the moan of doves – the peace before battles. The air is very still. An apple falls to the grass. It's an oak-apple. The world holds its breath. War is declared. It's a lovely evening . . .

GENERAL: But all at once –

GIRL: We're at the edge of a meadow. I am careful not to skitter – to whinny. Your thighs are warm, and you're pressing my flanks –

GENERAL: But all at once –

GIRL: Death pricks up her ears. Finger to her lips, it is she who is calling for silence. Goodness illuminates the world for the very last time. And even you forget that I am there . . .

18

GENERAL: But all at once –

GIRL: Do your own buttons up, General. The water lies motionless in the ponds. The wind itself awaits an order to unfurl.

GENERAL: But all at once . . .

GIRL: All at once? Hm? All at once? (*She seems to be at a loss for words.*) Ah yes: all at once, all is fire and sword. The widows! Miles of crêpe have to be woven for the standards. Wives and mothers remain dry-eyed behind their veils. The bells come tumbling down the bombed belfries. As I come round a bend in the road, a blue cloth startles me. I rear, but your gentle, heavy hand masters me, and my trembling ceases. I amble on. How I love you, my hero!

GENERAL: But . . . what about the dead? Aren't there any dead?

GIRL: The soldiers died kissing the standard. You were all triumph and tenderness. One evening, do you remember . . .

GENERAL: I was so tender that I began to snow. To snow on my men, to wind them in the softest of shrouds. To snow. Bérézina!

GIRL: At last Death goes into action. Lightly. She flits from soldier to soldier, deepening a wound here, dimming an eye there, tearing out an arm, opening an artery, discolouring a face, cutting short a cry – or a song – Death can do no more. Finally, at her last gasp, Death herself dead with fatigue – she grows drowsy, rests lightly on your shoulder – and falls fast asleep.

GENERAL: (*Drunk with joy*) Not yet, not yet – we mustn't get there yet – but when we do I know it's going to be magnificent. And the Sam Browne? Perfect!
(*He looks at himself in the mirror.*)
Waterloo! General! Man of war, in full dress. Behold me in my pure appearance. With no contingent at my back. Simply myself – I appear. If I have gone through wars without dying, through suffering without dying, if I have risen from the ranks without dying, it was only to reach this minute just before dying. (*He suddenly stops speaking: an idea seems to be troubling him.*) Tell me, Dove . . .

GIRL: Yes, sir?

GENERAL: How's the Chief of Police getting on?

(*The* GIRL *shakes her head.*)
Still nothing. Poor chap, he's losing his grip. And what about us – are we wasting our time?

GIRL: (*Imperiously*) Not at all. In any case, it's nothing to do with us. Carry on. You were saying: to reach this minute, just before dying . . . What comes next?

GENERAL: (*Hesitating*) Just before dying . . . when I shall be nothing but my image reflected to infinity in these mirrors. That's right, comb your mane, groom yourself. I like my filly to be well-groomed. Because, when the trumpets call, we shall descend, you and I – I on your back – to death and glory, for I shall die. It will really be a descent to the tomb.

GIRL: But General – you've been dead since yesterday.

GENERAL: I know . . . I know . . . a solemn, picturesque descent down unexpected stairways . . .

GIRL: For a dead general, you're very eloquent.

GENERAL: Eloquent because dead, talkative little horse! The voice you now hear – the lovely voice you now hear – is that of – Example. *I* am now no more than the image of what I was! Your turn now. Hang your head, and hide your eyes, I want to be General in solitude. Not for my sake, mind you, but for the sake of my image, and my image for the sake of its image, and so on. In short, we shall all be the image of each other. Dove, are you ready?
(*The* GIRL *nods.*)
Come on, then. Put on your bay-coloured dress, my little horse, my beautiful Spanish jennet. (*He puts the toy horse over her head. Then he cracks his whip.*) Hail! (*Saluting his reflection in the mirror.*) And farewell! And farewell! General!
(*He then lies back in the armchair, puts his feet up on another chair, and salutes the audience, holding himself as rigid as a corpse. The* GIRL *takes up her position in front of the chair and, without moving from the spot, makes the gestures of a walking horse.*)

GIRL: (*Solemnly and sadly*) The procession is under way . . . We are passing through the city . . . going along the river. I am sad. The sky is overcast. The people weep for their splendid hero who fell in battle . . .

GENERAL: (*With a start*) Dove!

20

GIRL: (*Looking around in tears*) Yes, General?

GENERAL: Tell them I died with my boots on! (*He resumes his pose.*)

(*Still walking on the spot, the* GIRL *sings Chopin's Funeral March: it is continued by an invisible brass band. In the distance the crackle of machine-gun fire.*)

SCENE 4

A room consisting of three panelled mirrors in which a LITTLE OLD MAN *is reflected. He is dressed as a tramp, though he is quite well-groomed, and he is standing motionless in the middle of the room.*

Near him, looking indifferent, is a very beautiful red-headed GIRL. *Leather corselet, leather boots. Beautiful naked thighs. Fur jacket. She is waiting for something. So is the* LITTLE OLD MAN. *He is nervous and impatient. The* GIRL *doesn't move. The* LITTLE OLD MAN *takes off his torn gloves with trembling hands. He takes a white handkerchief out of his pocket and wipes his face. He takes off his glasses. He folds them and puts them into a case, then puts the case into his pocket. He wipes his hands with his handkerchief.*

All the LITTLE OLD MAN's *movements are reflected in each of the mirrors (so three actors will be needed to play the parts of the reflections).*

Finally there are three knocks on the rear door. The redheaded GIRL *goes over to it. She says: 'Yes'. The door opens a little and* IRMA's *arm and hand come through the gap, holding a whip and a very dirty, shaggy wig. The* GIRL *takes them. The door shuts.*

The LITTLE OLD MAN's *face lights up. The redhead looks exaggeratedly cruel and haughty. She shoves the wig roughly on his head. The* LITTLE OLD MAN *takes a little bunch of artificial flowers out of his pocket. He holds it as if he were going to offer it to the* GIRL, *but she whips him and then lashes it out of his hand.*

The LITTLE OLD MAN's *face is illuminated with tenderness.*

A burst of machine-gun fire quite close.

The LITTLE OLD MAN *touches his wig.*

LITTLE OLD MAN: What about the lice?

GIRL: (*Brutally*) They're there, all right.

SCENE 5

A sort of vestibule, with a door protected by an iron grating. Heavy locks. Left, the first few steps of a staircase. Two YOUNG MEN *who look as if they are in still photographs: the first is near the top of the stairs and seems to be rushing up them, the second is crouching at the bottom, his hands on his knees, looking as if he is just about to follow suit. A third young man is smoking a cigarette and walking up and down the room.*

The three YOUNG MEN *(they are all about twenty) are very handsome. Long, dishevelled hair, falling over their eyes. The first is wearing boots, with an open-necked shirt, the second, shorts with a polo-neck sweater; the third has a red Spahi's burnous over his white tennis costume.*

This scene doesn't come to a halt. It simply crosses the stage very slowly from left to right.

SCENE 6

IRMA's *room. Very elegant. It is the original of the room that was reflected in the mirrors in the first three scenes. The same chandelier. Tall lace hangings suspended from the flies. Three armchairs. Large bay windows, left. Door right.* IRMA *is sitting at her dressing table, doing her accounts. Near her, a girl:* CARMEN. *A burst of machine-gun fire.*

CARMEN: (*Counting*) Twenty from the Bishop . . . twenty from the judge . . .

IRMA: (*Interrupting*) Still no Chief of Police?

CARMEN: Still no Chief of Police!

IRMA: Still? I can't understand it!

CARMEN: I know. Takes all sorts to make a world, but still no Chief of Police!
(*Pause.*)

IRMA: He'll be in a filthy temper when he gets here – if he gets here.
(*Pause.*)

CARMEN: Twenty from the General . . . twenty from the Beggar . . . thirty from the Little Shit . . .

22

IRMA: Don't call him that!

CARMEN: Sorry.

IRMA: I've told you before, Carmen, I won't have it!

CARMEN: (*Acidly*) Nobody's perfect!

IRMA: And I won't have any backchat either! I insist upon respect for my visitors. Vi-si-tors! I don't even allow myself, myself even, to call them clients.

(*Silence.*)

CARMEN: When I call them by their titles, Madam, I do it in a nice way. Even in my dreams I embroider a uniform on their images.

IRMA: (*Relenting*) I know. (*Smiling*) Mind you, when it comes to the one who has himself tethered to a stake . . .

CARMEN: I call him quite tenderly, Nanny Goat. Which is more or less what he manages to be for half an hour.

IRMA: (*As if in a dream*) Tenderly . . .! (*Pulling herself together*) Tenderly? Ah yes, I was forgetting you got quite 'tied up' with him.

CARMEN: (*Exploding*) You dare blame me for that?'

IRMA: (*Throwing a bundle of banknotes she is holding on to the dressing table*) On the contrary . . .

CARMEN: (*Toughly*) It's all right for you. Cash – every refinement!

IRMA: (*Sharply*) Don't be unjust, Carmen.

(*Pause.*)

(*Trying to placate her*) What eyes! You've been irritable for some time now, Carmen. I know this upheaval's getting on all our nerves, but things will quieten down soon. The sun will shine again. Mr George . . .

CARMEN: Oh, him.

IRMA: Don't you sneer at the Chief of Police. Fine mess we'd be in if it weren't for him. Yes, *we*, we're all in this together – all three of us.

(*A long silence.*)

What worries me most is that you're always so sad. (*Sounding wise.*) You've changed, Carmen. You started changing even before the revolution began.

CARMEN: There's nothing much left for me to do here, Madam Irma.

IRMA: (*Disconcerted*) But – I've put you in charge of my accounts.

23

You sit at my desk, and my entire life opens out before you. I haven't a secret left – and you're still not happy!

CARMEN: Obviously I'm grateful for your confidence, but . . . it's not the same.

IRMA: Do you really miss – 'that'?

(CARMEN *says nothing.*)

Oh, come now, Carmen – when you used to climb up on to that snow-covered rock and stand by the rose bush with its yellow paper roses – which I must remember to return to the prop cellar, by the way – and when the cripple you'd miraculously healed fainted away at your apparition, you didn't really take yourself seriously, did you Carmen? Did you?

(*A short silence.*)

CARMEN: When our sessions are over, Madam Irma, you never allow us to talk about them. So you've no idea how we really feel. You observe it all from a distance, Madam, but if you'd ever even once worn the dress and the blue veil, if you'd been the penitent in sackcloth and ashes, or the General's mare, or the Farmer's daughter tumbled in the hay . . .

IRMA: (*Shocked*) Me!

CARMEN: Yes, you, Madam Irma. Or the chambermaid in the pink apron, or the archduchess being deflowered by the policeman, or . . . Well, I won't go through the entire cast list, but if you had, even once, then you'd know what it does to a girl's soul, and that she's got to have a sense of humour to protect herself. But you won't even let us talk about it amongst ourselves. You're afraid that if we so much as smile, let alone joke . . .

IRMA: (*Very harshly*) I certainly won't have any joking. A laugh, or even a smile, and the whole thing's on the floor. Where there's a smile, there's a doubt. The customers like their ceremonies solemn.

CARMEN: The visitors.

IRMA: The visitors. Mine's a strict house, mine is.

CARMEN: Then don't be surprised if we're sad.

IRMA: I let you play cards.

CARMEN: Anyway, I'm thinking about my daughter.

(*A bell rings.* IRMA *gets up and goes over to the strange piece of*

24

furniture on the left – a sort of switchboard with a kind of
eyepiece, receiver and a lot of switches. She goes on speaking
while she presses a switch and looks through the eyepiece.)

IRMA: Every time I ask you a question that's the slightest bit
intimate you put on that hard look and chuck your daughter
in my face. Do you still want to go and see her? You fool, it's
a bloodbath between this house and the country: fire and
sword, death and destruction. I'm beginning to wonder if
they even got Mr George on his way here . . .
(*The bell rings again.* IRMA *flicks one switch up and another*
down.)
. . . though a Chief of Police usually knows how to look after
himself. (*She pulls a watch out of her blouse and looks at the*
time.) He's late.

CARMEN: Your gentlemen aren't afraid of the bullets when they
want to come here. And I'm not afraid of the bullets when I
want to see my daughter.

IRMA: Aren't afraid! Fear excites them. Their nostrils dilate –
they sniff the orgies going on behind the wall of fire. Your
orgies go on in your heart . . .

CARMEN: But they don't help, Madam. My daughter loves me.

IRMA: You're like a fairy godmother to her – a perfumed lady
who comes bearing gifts from afar. She thinks you come
from heaven. (*She bursts out laughing.*) That's really over the
top! That's marvellous – at last someone thinks my brothel –
which is hell – is heaven! Your kid thinks it's heaven. (*She*
laughs.) Are you going to make a whore of her when she
grows up?

CARMEN: Madam Irma!

IRMA: You're right. I must leave you to your sentimental brothel,
your precious pink knocking shop, your secret whorehouse
. . . You think I'm cruel, don't you? The revolution's getting
on my nerves, too. You may not realize it, Carmen, but there
are times when I get frightened, really frightened.
Sometimes I feel the main aim of the revolution is not so
much to take the palace as to sack my studios. I'm afraid,
Carmen. And I've tried everything – even prayer. (*She*
smiles.) Like the cripple you used to heal so miraculously.
Have I hurt your feelings?

25

CARMEN: (*Positively*) Twice a week, on Tuesdays and Fridays. I used to have to appear as the Immaculate Conception of Lourdes to a Midland Counties bank clerk. All that meant to you was money in the till, but to me, a believer, it was . . .

IRMA: (*Amazed*) You agreed to do it. You didn't seem to mind . . .

CARMEN: Mind? I was happy!

IRMA: Well, then? What was so bad about it?

CARMEN: I saw the effect I had on him. I'd watch him go into a kind of fit, break out in a cold sweat, I'd hear the rattle in his throat . . .

IRMA: All right, all right. He doesn't come any more. No he doesn't, come to think of it. I wonder why not? Because of the danger, I suppose. He could be dead. (*Pause*.) Perhaps his wife found out.

CARMEN: Who cares?

IRMA: Get on with those books.

CARMEN: Your accounts will never replace my apparition. It had become as real as at Lourdes. All I can think of now is my daughter, Madam Irma. She's in a real garden.

IRMA: You can't possibly get there, and before long the garden will be in your heart anyway.

CARMEN: Don't say such things!

IRMA: (*Inexorably*) The town is full of corpses. All the roads are cut off. Even the peasants are going over to the revolution. Goodness knows why. Contagion, perhaps. The revolution's an epidemic. It has the same sacred fatality. Whatever happens, we're going to be more and more isolated. The rebels are anti-clergy, anti-army, anti-law and they're even against me, Irma, mother of bawds and madam of brothels. As for you – you'll be killed and disembowelled, and your daughter will be adopted by a virtuous rebel. We shan't any of us escape.

(*A sudden bell.* IRMA *runs over to the switchboard and looks and listens as before.*)

CARMEN: Is it the Chief of Police?

IRMA: No. It's Studio 24 – the desert room. What's the trouble? (*She watches carefully. A long silence.*)

CARMEN: (*Who has sat down at* IRMA's *dressing table, and is going*

26

on with the accounts. Without looking up) Is it the Foreign
Legion?

IRMA: *(With her eye still glued to the machine)* Yes, it's the heroic
Legionary who falls in the desert. And that idiot Rachael has
hit him in the ear with an arrow. He might have been
disfigured for life. Still, what an idea, getting her to pretend
to be an Arab, and then dying – if that's what you call it –
standing to attention on a sandcastle!
(A silence. She watches carefully.)
Ah, Rachael's giving him first aid. She's making him a
bandage and he's looking very pleased. *(Extremely interested)*
My! – he really does seem to like it. I shouldn't be surprised
if he decides to change his script: from now on he'll probably
want to die in a military hospital being tucked in by a nurse
. . . Another costume to buy . . . Expenses, expenses . . .
(Suddenly worried) Oh, I don't like that. I don't like that at
all. I'm getting really worried about Rachael. She'd better
not do a Chantal on me. *(Turning round, to* CARMEN*)* Any
news of Chantal, by the way?

CARMEN: No. None at all.

IRMA: *(Turning back to the machine)* What's the matter with this
bloody thing! What's he saying? He's explaining . . . she's
listening . . . she understands . . . I'm afraid he understands
too. No, I don't like the way they're looking at each other at
all – it's much too clear-eyed. You see the dangers of being
over-conscientious. It would be a catastrophe if my clients
started exchanging friendly smiles with my girls. It'd be an
even greater catastrophe than if they fell in love with one
another.
(The bell rings again. She flicks another switch and watches.)
False alarm. It's the plumber on his way out.

CARMEN: Which one?

IRMA: The real one.

CARMEN: Which one is the real one?

IRMA: The one who mends the taps.

CARMEN: Is the other one a phoney one?

IRMA: *(Shrugs her shoulders, and presses the first switch)* Hm, just as
I thought, those two or three drops of blood from his ear
have inspired him. Now she's kissing it better. He'll be in

great form at his embassy tomorrow morning.

CARMEN: He's married, isn't he?

IRMA: I usually make it a rule not to talk about my visitors' private lives. The Grand Balcony is known all over the world as the most sophisticated and the most respectable House of Illusions . . .

CARMEN: Respectable?

IRMA: Discreet. Still, to be frank – you inquisitive little thing, you: they're almost all married.

CARMEN: When they're with their wives – do they still carry with them – I mean when they're making love to their wives – do they still carry with them the joys they find in a brothel . . .?

IRMA: Bitch.

CARMEN: Sorry . . . a house of illusions, at the back of their minds, very far back and very tiny, but still there.

IRMA: Possibly. They must do, I suppose. Yes. Like a fairy light left over from last year's carnival waiting for the next – or, perhaps, like an imperceptible glimmer at the imperceptible window of an imperceptible castle which they can turn into a blaze of light at the flick of a switch whenever they want to go there, to rest.

(*The crackle of machine-gun fire.*)

Do you hear that? It's getting nearer. They're still after me.

CARMEN: Must be nice in a real house though, isn't it?

IRMA: (*Getting more and more frightened*) They'll have surrounded the brothel by the time George gets here. One thing to remember – if we ever get out of this mess – is that neither the walls nor the windows are sufficiently padded. In the house we can hear everything that goes on in the street, which means that in the street they can hear everything that goes on in the house.

CARMEN: (*Still pensive*) In a real house . . . it must be really nice . . .

IRMA: Who knows? But Carmen, Carmen, if all my girls started getting ideas like that into their heads, it'd be the ruin of the brothel. I believe you really do miss playing that apparition. Listen – there's something I can do for you. I did promise it to Regina, but I'll give it to you instead. If you want it. Someone rang me yesterday and asked for a Saint Theresa . . .

(*Silence.*)

Yes, well, of course, a Saint Theresa is a bit of a come-down
from an Immaculate Conception, but it's not that bad . . .
(*Silence.*)
Say something: it's for a banker. He's very clean, you know.
Easy to please.

CARMEN: I really loved my dress, and my veil, and my rose bush.

IRMA: There's a rose bush in the Saint Theresa too. Think about
it.
(*Silence.*)

CARMEN: What'll be the authentic detail?

IRMA: The ring. He's got it all worked out. The wedding ring.
You know that nuns all wear wedding rings, because they're
God's brides.
(CARMEN *makes a gesture of astonishment.*)
They do, you know. That's how he'll know he's got a real
nun.

CARMEN: And the phoney detail?

IRMA: Same as usual: black lace under the homespun skirt. Come
on, say you'll do it. You're his type, you know – he likes
them gentle. He'll be pleased.

CARMEN: You're really kind to care about him like that.

IRMA: It's you I care about.

CARMEN: When I said you were kind, I wasn't being sarcastic,
Madam Irma. The good thing about your house is the
consolation it offers. You set the stage for their secret
dramas, yet you have your feet on the ground. You rake in all
the money and they wake up. It must be a terrible
awakening! And no sooner it's over but it has to start again.

IRMA: Lucky for me.

CARMEN: All over again! And always the same adventure. They
never want to break out of it.

IRMA: You don't understand the half of it. I can see it through
their eyes: when it's over, they're clear-headed again. All of a
sudden they can understand mathematics. They love their
children and their country. Just like you.

CARMEN: (*Boastfully*) I'm a colonel's daughter . . .

IRMA: I know. No brothel should ever be without one. But just
think what the Judge, the General and the Bishop are in real
life . . .

CARMEN: Which ones are you talking about?

IRMA: The real ones.

CARMEN: Which ones are the real ones? The ones we have here?

IRMA: The other ones. In life their role is to keep the show going, trailing it through the mud of everyday reality. Here, theatre and appearance keep their purity: the ceremony remains intact.

CARMEN: The ceremony I dream of –

IRMA: (*Interrupting her*) Is to forget theirs.

CARMEN: Do you blame me?

IRMA: And theirs is to forget yours. They love their children, too. Afterwards.

(The bell rings again, as before. IRMA *has been sitting near the machine all the time, and she turns round, looks through the eyepiece and puts the receiver to her ear.* CARMEN *goes back to her accounts.)*

CARMEN: (*Without looking up*) Is it the Chief of Police?

IRMA: No. It's the waiter. He's only just arrived, but he's going to start complaining again . . . there he goes. He's furious because Elyane's got a white apron.

CARMEN: I warned you; he likes pink ones.

IRMA: Go and buy one in the market tomorrow, if it's open. Oh, and while you're at it, buy a feather duster for the railwayman. A green feather duster.

CARMEN: I hope Elyane doesn't forget to drop the tip on the floor. He insists on a real revolt, and dirty glasses.

IRMA: They all want everything to be as real as possible . . . Minus an indefinable something, so that it's not really real.

CARMEN: (*Turning round*) A bishop keeps his prestige in the eyes of the world whatever happens. I know the man who plays the Nanny Goat is a phoney count. He doesn't know I know. But, believe me, when I call him by his title, I believe in it.

IRMA: It was I who decided to christen my establishment a House of Illusions, Carmen, but I'm only its director, and everyone, when he rings my bell, comes in with his own carefully worked out, ready-made script. All I have to do is rent the hall and provide the props, actors and actresses. I've managed to get my house off the ground, Carmen dear – you see what I mean? I cut adrift a long time ago, and it took off.

I cut the cables. It's airborne. Or if you like, it's floating through the sky, and taking me with it. Well, darling – you don't mind my sounding a bit affectionate, do you? – it's a tradition that every brothel Madam has a slight partiality for one of her young ladies . . .

CARMEN: I had noticed, Madam. And I too, sometimes. (*She gives* IRMA *a long, languid look.*)

IRMA: (*Standing up and looking at her*) I'm a bit confused, Carmen . . .

(*Long silence.*)

Where were we? But darling, when I call myself – in my heart of hearts, secretly, but with total accuracy – a brothel-keeper, darling, when secretly, in silence, I repeat to myself in the silence: you're a cunt seller, a fuck and suck merchant, then darling, everything (*She suddenly becomes lyrical*) – everything becomes airborne: chandeliers, mirrors, carpets, pianos, caryatides – and my studios, my famous studios: my Harvest Room, with its rustic scenes, my Torture Room, splashed with blood and tears, my Throne Room, with its leopard-patterned velvet, my hall of mirrors, my State Room, my Perfumed Garden, my Urinal Cottage, my Amphitrite's Glade, my Funeral Parlour, with its marble urns, my Moonlight Terrace – it all becomes airborne. Studios! – Ah! I was forgetting the Beggars' and Tramps' Salon, where filth and poverty are glorified. As I was saying: studios, girls . . . (*Checking herself*) And, of course, the most magnificent of all, the culminating point, the crowning glory of the edifice – that's if it's ever actually completed – my Studio of Solemn Death, the Tomb! the Mausoleum . . . As I was saying: studios, girls, crystals, lace, balcony, the whole lot goes sodding off – up into the blue, and takes me with it! (*A long silence. The two women are standing facing each other: neither moves.*)

CARMEN: You do talk nicely.

IRMA: (*Modestly*) I did stay at school till I was fourteen.

CARMEN: I can see that. My father, the artillery colonel –

IRMA: (*Correcting her sharply*) Cavalry, dear.

CARMEN: Sorry. That's right. The cavalry colonel – wanted me to have a good education. Alas . . . But, you, you've made it.

You have been able to organize a fabulous theatre around your loveliness, a celebration whose splendour envelops and masks you from the world. Your whoredom requires this grandeur. But what about me – am I to have only myself and be only myself? No, Madam, with the help of the vice and misery of men, I too have had my hour of glory. You could see me from here – with your ear to the receiver and your eye to the spy-hole – you could see me standing erect, sovereign, and at the same time sweet, matriarchal, yet so feminine, with the pink paper roses, my heel on the cardboard snake; and you could also see the Midlands Counties bank clerk on his knees before me, fainting at my apparition.
Unfortunately he had his back to you, so you weren't aware of his look of ecstasy, or the wild pounding of my heart. My blue veil, my blue dress, my blue apron, my blue eyes –

IRMA: Brown!

CARMEN: They were blue, that day. For him I was heaven incarnate descended to touch his brow. He sang hymns to me, compounded me with his beloved colour, and when he carried me to the bed it was into the blue that he penetrated. (*She sighs*.) But I shall never appear again.

IRMA: I did offer you Saint Theresa.

CARMEN: I haven't prepared that one, Madam Irma. I have to know what the customer's going to want, don't I? Has it all been worked out?

IRMA: Any self-respecting whore should be capable of handling *any* sort of situation . . . You don't mind me calling you a whore, do you darling? Seeing we've gone this far, we might as well talk man to man.

CARMEN: I am one of your whores, Madam, and I flatter myself that I am one of your best whores. In a single evening I can . . .

IRMA: I know your performances. I've seen them. But when you get so excited at the word whore, when you keep repeating it to yourself and boasting of it as if it were a title, it isn't quite the same as when I use the word to express a function. Still you're right, darling, to extol your profession, to glory in it. Rub it, make it shine, let it shine upon you, it's the only thing you have. (*Affectionately*) I'll do everything I can to help you . . . You're not only the purest jewel in my diadem of girls, you're also the only one I'm really fond of. Stay with me. How could you leave now – now, when death – real, final death – is at my door, waiting beneath my windows? (*They look at each other*.) Let's get back to our accounts, shall we?

CARMEN: Counting the sailor and the short-timers, it comes to 320 all told.

IRMA: Good. The more killing there is in the suburbs, the more men I get in my studios.

CARMEN: Men?

IRMA: (*After a silence*) Some of them are. They're attracted by my unchanging mirrors and chandeliers, for the others heroism is a substitute for women.

CARMEN: (*Bitterly*) Women?

IRMA: What else should I call you, my Amazons, my sterile beauties? Their seed never ripens in you, and yet – if you weren't there?

CARMEN: You have your rites, Madam Irma, your ceremonies . . .

IRMA: Don't talk about them. They're the cause of my sadness and melancholy, those glacial games. It's just as well I have my jewellery. Though even that's in danger now. I could lose the lot if I'm not careful. You won't tell Arthur, will you?

CARMEN: What about?

IRMA: The accounts.
(*There is a knock.* IRMA *starts*.)
(*Speaking more softly*) Talk of the devil . . . (*To* CARMEN) Quick, make up your mind. Will you stay? (CARMEN *doesn't answer*.) Say you will. A grey homespun dress, Carmen, a bunch of roses . . .
(*More knocks at the door*.)

CARMEN: But Madam, I believe in it . . .
(*More knocks, even more peremptory*.)

IRMA: (*To* CARMEN) Idiot . . .! Come in!
(*The door opens. Enter the* TORTURER *whom, from now on, we shall call* ARTHUR. *He is dressed as the classic pimp: light grey suit, white felt hat, etc. He is putting the finishing touches to his tie*.)

IRMA: That was quick. Finished already.

ARTHUR: Yes. The old boy's buttoning up. He's knocked out. Two goes in half an hour.

33

IRMA: I hope you didn't hit Marlyse too hard. Last time the poor kid was laid up for two whole days.

ARTHUR: Don't come the heart-of-gold stuff. Last time, and tonight, she got what was coming to her – the cash and the lash! Right on. The banker wants to see her back striped – I stripe.

IRMA: I hope you don't get any pleasure out of it.

ARTHUR: Not with her; you're the only one I love. But a job's a job. And I'm a conscientious worker.

IRMA: (*Authoritatively*) I'm not jealous of the girl, I just don't want you damaging the personnel; it's getting harder and harder to replace.

ARTHUR: I did try two or three times to draw the marks on her back with purple paint, but it didn't work. The old boy inspects her when he arrives and insists I hand her over in good shape.

IRMA: Paint? Who gave you permission to use paint?

ARTHUR: (*Shrugging his shoulders*) What's one illusion more or less! I was only trying to help. Anyway nowadays, I flog, she screams, and he crawls.

IRMA: By the way, tell her to scream quieter, will you? The house is being watched.

ARTHUR: I know. All the northern districts fell last night. It's a bore; but the Judge will have his screams.

IRMA: The Bishop's less of a problem. He's content to forgive sins.

CARMEN: He still insists on our committing them first, though. No, the best of the lot is the one you have to swaddle up and spank; then you whip him, then you coddle him, and then he snores.

ARTHUR: Who does the coddling? (*To* CARMEN) You? Do you give him the breast?

CARMEN:(*Dryly*) I'm a conscientious worker too.

ARTHUR: Perhaps the young lady would care to work on me.

IRMA: Leave Carmen alone. She's suffering. (*To* CARMEN) What about Saint Theresa, then; will you do it?

CARMEN: (*Querulously*) Give me time to think.

ARTHUR: (*Bowing ironically to* CARMEN) Her ladyship's cashier? No, pardon me: her accountant?

CARMEN: You can't afford to make jokes in that costume, Mr
    Arthur. A pimp grins, he never smiles.
IRMA: She's right!
ARTHUR: How much did you take today?
IRMA: (*On the defensive*) Carmen and I haven't finished the
    accounts yet.
ARTHUR: I have. The way I work it out it'll be a good two hundred.
IRMA: Could be. But you needn't worry. I don't cheat.
ARTHUR: I know you don't, my love, but I just can't help myself:
    the figures will keep running through my head. Two hundred!
    All the wars, revolutions, machine-guns, frost, hail, rain and
    shit in the world won't stop them! On the contrary. People are
    killing each other out there, the shop's being watched, the
    town's on fire, but they still come charging right on in just the
    same. Anyway, I'm all right: me, I've got you on the premises,
    my lovely, but if I hadn't . . .
IRMA: (*Bluntly*) You'd be shitting your pants in a cellar,
    somewhere.
ARTHUR: (*Ambigously*) I'd be doing the same as the rest of you, my
    love. You aren't forgetting my little percentage, are you?
IRMA: I give you quite enough to get by on.
ARTHUR: But my love! I've ordered my silk shirts. And do you
    know what sort of silk? And what colour?
IRMA: (*Tenderly*) All right, that'll do. Not in front of Carmen.
ARTHUR: And why not? Do you know what silk it is?
IRMA: Darling! The idea that Carmen will know that your chest
    . . . in the silk of my blouses . . . Oh darling . . . hush . . .
ARTHUR: Is it all right, then?
IRMA: We haven't done the accounts yet.
ARTHUR: I'll tell you something else. You ought to have seen the
    shirtmaker's face – when I told him they'd got to button on the
    left. As if they were for you!
IRMA: My love!
ARTHUR: Well? Is it yes?
IRMA: Yes!
ARTHUR: How much?
IRMA: (*Pulling herself together*) We'll see. I've got to finish the
    accounts with Carmen. (*Ingratiatingly*) I'll make it as much as
    I can. Now you simply must go and meet George.

35

ARTHUR: (*With insolent irony*) I beg your pardon, beloved?

IRMA: (*Curtly*) You've got to go and meet George. All the way to Police Headquarters, if need be: and tell him that I'm absolutely relying on him.

ARTHUR: (*Slightly worried*) You must be joking . . .?

IRMA: (*Suddenly very authoritative*) The tone of my last remark should convince you otherwise. I'm not playing any more – not the same part, anyway. And you can stop playing the weak, vicious pimp. Do what I tell you, but first the scent spray. (*To* CARMEN, *who is bringing it*) Give it to him. (*To* ARTHUR) On your knees!

ARTHUR: (*Kneels on one knee and sprays* IRMA) In the street . . .? On my own . . .? Me . . .?

IRMA: (*Standing in front of him*) I must find out what's become of George. I've got to have protection.

ARTHUR: You've got me!

IRMA: (*Shrugging her shoulders*) I've got to protect my jewellery, my studios and my girls. The Chief of Police ought to have been here half an hour ago . . .

ARTHUR: (*Pathetic*) Me, in the street . . .? But they're shooting . . . it's hailing bullets . . . (*pointing to his suit*) I put this on specially to stay in, to walk down your corridors and look at myself in the mirrors. *And* so's you could see me dressed as a pimp . . . I've got nothing but silk to protect me . . .

IRMA: (*To* CARMEN) Give me my bracelets, Carmen . . . (*To* ARTHUR) And you – spray!

ARTHUR: I'm not made for the great outdoors. I've lived too long within your four walls . . . My skin won't be able to stand the fresh air . . . if I only had a little veil . . .! What if someone recognizes me . . .?

IRMA: (*Irritated, pivoting round as she is being sprayed*) Hug the walls. (*Pause.*) Take the revolver.

ARTHUR: (*Terrified*) What, me?

IRMA: In your pocket.

ARTHUR: My pocket! But just imagine if I have to shoot . . .

IRMA: (*Gently*) You're so full of yourself, aren't you? Sated.

ARTHUR: Sated, yes . . . (*Pause.*) Sated . . . sedated . . . but if I go out into the street . . .

IRMA: (*Authoritatively, but still gently*) You're right. No revolver.

Take your hat off, anyway.

IRMA: If you were the only man in my life we'd be in a nice mess. Now go! And don't be long. You've got a session this evening. Remember?

ARTHUR: (*Who was on his way to the door*) This evening? Another one? What is it?

IRMA: I thought I'd told you: a corpse.

ARTHUR: Charming! What am I supposed to do with it?

IRMA: Nothing. You stay still and get buried. You'll be able to have a rest.

ARTHUR: Ah, because I'm the . . . Great! And who's the customer? A new one?

IRMA: (*Mysteriously*) a VIP, and don't ask any more questions. Go!

ARTHUR: (*Starts to go out, then hesitates, and asks timidly*) Don't I get a kiss?

IRMA: When you come back. If you come back.

ARTHUR: Bitch! (*He turns round and smiles.*) Adorable bitch! (*Exits.*)

IRMA: Dress me.

CARMEN: What are you going to wear?

IRMA: My cream negligée.

(CARMEN *opens the door of the wardrobe and takes out the negligée, while* IRMA *starts undoing her suit.*)

Tell me, my Carmen . . . Chantal?

CARMEN: Chantal, Madam?

IRMA: Yes. Tell me: what do you know about Chantal?

CARMEN: I've had a word with all the girls: Rosina, Elyane, Florence and Marlyse. I'll tell you what they reported, but I didn't find out much. The time to spy on the people is beforehand. It's more difficult when the fighting's actually begun. For one thing, the two sides are more clearly defined: you can choose. But when it's just peace, everything's too vague. You don't exactly know who you're betraying or even if you're betraying. There's absolutely no news about Chantal. No one even knows whether she still exists.

IRMA: Yes, but tell me – didn't you have any scruples?

CARMEN: No. To enter a brothel is to renounce the world. Here I am, here I stay. My reality consists of your mirrors, and your

37

orders – and of passions. Which jewels will you wear?

IRMA: The pearls. My jewels. They're all I've got that's real. In the certain knowledge that everything else is phoney, I have my jewels like other people have a little girl in a country garden. Who is a traitor? You hesitate . . .

CARMEN: None of the girls trust me. I listen to what they tell me. I pass it on to you. You pass it on to the police. They check it out . . . Personally, I don't know a thing.

IRMA: Prudent, aren't you? Give me a handkerchief.

CARMEN: (*Bringing a lace handkerchief*) No, I'm not prudent. Looking at it from here – where men come to lay themselves bare – in every way – life seems to me so remote, so fathomless, that it has all the unreality of a film or the birth of Christ in a manger. When a man so far forgets himself in one of your salons as to tell me: 'We're going to take the Arsenal tomorrow,' I feel as if I were reading some obscene graffiti. His action has become just as mad, just as . . . voluminous . . . as the acts people describe in a certain way on a certain sort of wall . . .

(*Same bell as before.* IRMA *looks through the eye-piece.*)

CARMEN: Is it the Chief of Police?

IRMA: No. It's Christ leaving. With all his stuff in a suitcase. I've never been able to understand why he has to get tied to the cross with his own ropes. Maybe they're consecrated? Where on earth does he put them when he gets home? Who cares?

(*A burst of machine-gun fire.*)

Did you hear that?

CARMEN: The army's putting up a good fight.

IRMA: The rebels are putting up an even better one. And we're right under the cathedral walls, the Archbishop's Palace is just around the corner. I won't say there's a price on my head – that would be too much to ask, but it's known that all sorts of prominent people come to my little suppers. So I'm one of their targets. And there are no men in the house.

CARMEN: Arthur will be back soon.

IRMA: He isn't a man, he's one of my props.

CARMEN: Assuming the worst . . .

IRMA: That the rebels win? I'll have had it. They're workers. No imagination. Prudes – possibly even chaste.

38

CARMEN: They'll soon get used to bit of debauchery. Wait till they start getting bored.

IRMA: They won't get bored. They won't allow themselves to. No! I'm their number one target. It's different for you. In every revolution there's the fanatical prostitute who sings the battle hymn and turns herself back into a virgin. That'll probably be you or Chantal. The others will piously carry drink to the dying. After which . . . they'll marry you off. Would you like to be married?

CARMEN: Orange blossom . . . a veil . . .

IRMA: Wonderful. To you marriage means masquerade! Darling, you really are one of us! No, I can't imagine you married, either. Anyway, what they're really interested in is murdering us. We shall die a beautiful death, Carmen. It'll be terrible, and sumptuous. They'll break into my studios, smash my crystals, slash my brocades, slit our throats . . .

CARMEN: They'll have pity . . .

IRMA: No. Knowing they're committing sacrilege will make them even more violent. Booted and helmeted, or in their filthy cloth caps, they'll destroy us with fire and sword. It'll be sublime, we have no right to aspire to any other end – and you're thinking of leaving . . .

CARMEN: But Madam Irma . . .

IRMA: Yes. When the house is about to go up in flames, when the rose is about to be violated by the sword – all you can think of, Carmen, is running away.

CARMEN: I may have thought of taking a day or two off, but you know perfectly well why, don't you?

IRMA: Your daughter? But your daughter's dead . . .

CARMEN: Madam!

IRMA: Dead or alive, your daughter's dead. Think of her charming grave, with its daisies and artificial wreaths, at the bottom of a garden . . . and think of that garden in your heart, where you'll be able to tend it . . .

CARMEN: I'd have liked to have seen her again.

IRMA: You'll keep her image in the image of a garden, and keep the garden – in your heart, under Saint Theresa's blazing robe. And you hesitate? I offer you the most sublime of deaths, and you hesitate? Are you a coward?

CARMEN: You know I'm devoted to you . . .

IRMA: Then you'll stay? I'll teach you figures! Marvellous figures
– we'll spend whole nights transcribing them in the most
beautiful calligraphy.

CARMEN: (*Gently*) There's a war on. A civil war. You said
yourself the hordes were advancing . . .

IRMA: (*Triumphantly*) The hordes! But *we* have our cohorts, our
armies, our militias, legions, battalions, ships, heralds,
bugles and trumpets, our colours, oriflammes, standards and
banners . . . And you're trembling? But darling, all isn't lost.
We shall crush them. George is still in complete control –
providing he can get through.

CHIEF OF POLICE: (*Entering*) A Chief of Police always manages
to get through. No, no, don't go, Carmen. I like your being
here.
(*He keeps his hat and coat on, and his cigar in his mouth, but
bows to* IRMA, *and kisses her hand.*)
Sweet warmth, soft fragrance . . . (*Kissing* IRMA's *hand*) Such
beauty!

IRMA: (*Breathlessly*) I'm in such a state. I'm still shivering. I knew
you were on your way, so I knew you were in danger. I was
waiting for you – trembling, perfuming myself – put your
hand here (*On her breast*).

CHIEF OF POLICE: Hang on! Hang on! There's a war on,
remember. You were saying?

IRMA: Sod!

CHIEF OF POLICE: Right! So let's stop playing about, shall we.
The situation is deteriorating every minute – it isn't
desperate yet, but it soon will be – thank God! The Palace is
surrounded. The Queen's in hiding. It's a miracle I got
through at all what with the fighting and bloodshed. Out
there the revolution's tragic and joyous – not like this house
where everybody's dying by inches. It's all or nothing for
me, today. By tonight I'll either be in my grave or on a
pedestal. So whether I love you or whether I desire you isn't
of the slightest importance. How's everything going,
anyway?

IRMA: Marvellously. I've had some really great performances.

CHIEF OF POLICE: (*Impatiently*) What sort?

IRMA: Carmen has a genius for describing things. Ask her.

CHIEF OF POLICE: (*To* CARMEN) Well, Carmen?

CARMEN: Well, Sir. We still have the pillars of state: the Bishop, the Judge, the General.

CHIEF OF POLICE: (*Ironically*) Our heraldic allegories, our talking symbols. But you haven't had – by any chance this week . . . I mean . . . is there, perhaps . . .

CARMEN: A new theme?

CHIEF OF POLICE: Yes!

CARMEN: Of course, as there is every week.

(*The* CHIEF OF POLICE *makes a gesture indicating curiosity.*) This time it's a baby who gets slapped, spanked, and then tucked up: he cries, and you comfort him.

CHIEF OF POLICE: (*Impatiently*) Good. But . . .

CARMEN: He's charming, Sir. And so sad!

CHIEF OF POLICE: (*Irritably*) Is that all?

CARMEN: And so sweet when you take him out of his swaddling clothes . . .

CHIEF OF POLICE: (*With mounting fury*) Are you trying to take the piss out of me, Carmen?

CARMEN: I beg your pardon, Sir?

CHIEF OF POLICE: (*Exploding*) Has there or has there not been a simulacrum?

CARMEN: (*Bewildered*) Simulacrum?

CHIEF OF POLICE: Yes! Idiot! A simulacrum of the Chief of Police?

(*A very heavy silence.*)

IRMA: The time isn't ripe, my dear. Your function isn't noble enough yet to offer dreamers a consoling image that would enshrine them. Perhaps because it lacks illustrious ancestors? No, my love . . . you'll just have to face it: your image hasn't yet acceded to the brothel liturgy.

CHIEF OF POLICE: Who *does* get represented?

IRMA: You know very well – you've got your records: (*Counting on her fingers*) there are two kings of England, each with different rites and coronation ceremonies – an admiral going down on the bridge of his sinking destroyer, an Algerian dey surrendering, a fireman putting out a fire, a housewife coming back from market, a pickpocket, the victim of an armed robbery, bound and gagged and being beaten up, a Saint Sebastian, a farmer in his barn . . . there's no Chief of Police . . . nor colonial administrator, but there is a missionary dying on the cross, and Christ in person.

CHIEF OF POLICE: (*After a silence*) You're forgetting the mechanic.

IRMA: He doesn't come any more. He screwed in so many screws he practically made a whole machine. Which might actually have worked.

CHIEF OF POLICE: So none of your customers has ever had the idea . . . the remotest idea . . . even at the back of his mind . . .

IRMA: Never. I know you've been doing your best: you've tried both love and hate, but glory eludes you.

CHIEF OF POLICE: (*Forcefully*) Look, my image is growing every day. It's becoming colossal. I see it reflected in everything around me. And you stand there and tell me you've never seen it represented here.

IRMA: I shouldn't see it, even if it were celebrated here. The ceremonies are private.

CHIEF OF POLICE: Liar. You've got judas-holes everywhere. Every wall and every mirror is rigged. You listen to their sighs over here, and to the echo of their groans over there. You don't need me to tell you that brothel tricks are primarily mirror tricks. (*Very sadly*) Still no simulacrum! I shall force my image to detach itself from me, to penetrate, to violate your studios, to be reflected, to increase and multiply. Irma, I'm feeling the weight of my function. It will appear to me, here, in the terrible sun of Pleasure and Death.

IRMA: You'll have to do some more killing, George dear.

CHIEF OF POLICE: I'm doing as much as I can already. People fear me more and more.

IRMA: Not enough. You must plunge deeper into darkness, blood and shit.

CHIEF OF POLICE: I tell you I'm doing my best!

IRMA: (*In sudden anguish*) To kill whatever may be left of our love.

CHIEF OF POLICE: That's dead already.

IRMA: Some victory! Then you'll have to go on killing.

CHIEF OF POLICE: (*Extremely irritated*) I tell you – I'm doing everything I can. At the same time I've got to show the nation that I'm a leader, a legislator, a builder . . .

IRMA: (*Worried*) You're crazy. Unless you really do think you're an empire-builder – in which case, you're crazy.

CHIEF OF POLICE: (*With conviction*) When the revolution has been crushed, and crushed by me, and I have the nation behind me, and the Queen calls on me – nothing, but nothing, will be able to stop me. Only then will you see who I am now. (*Musing*) Yes, my dear, I want to build an empire – so that, in exchange, the empire will build me –

IRMA: A tomb –

CHIEF OF POLICE: (*Slightly taken aback*) And why not? Doesn't every conqueror have his tomb? Well then? Why not me? (*Excitably*) Alexandria! I shall have my tomb, Irma. And when they lay the foundation stone, you'll have a front seat.

IRMA: Thanks. Put the kettle on, will you, Carmen.

CHIEF OF POLICE: Just a minute. What do *you* think of the idea, Carmen?

CARMEN: That you want your life to be one long funeral, Sir.

CHIEF OF POLICE: (*Aggressively*) What else is life?

CARMEN: I never go out, Sir.

CHIEF OF POLICE: Quite. But you seem to know everything, so tell me: what have you observed? Here, in this sumptuous theatre, where there's always some drama being performed – like there's always a Mass being celebrated somewhere – what have you observed?

CARMEN: (*After a slight hesitation*) Only one thing of any importance, or worth mentioning, Sir: without the thighs it previously contained, a pair of trousers hanging over a chair is beautiful. Emptied of our little old men, our costumes are deathly sad. They're the vestments they lay over the catafalques of high dignitaries. All they do is cover corpses that never finish dying, and yet . . .

IRMA: That's not what the Chief of Police asked you, Carmen.

CHIEF OF POLICE: Don't stop her, my dear. I'm used to Carmen's speeches by now. (*To* CARMEN) And yet . . .

CARMEN: And yet the joy in their eyes when they see those

43

phoney costumes really is – I know I'm right – really is – the flash of innocence.

CHIEF OF POLICE: People accuse our house of sending them to Death.

(*A bell suddenly rings.* IRMA *starts.* A SILENCE.)

IRMA: They've opened the door. Who on earth can it be at this time of night? (*To* CARMEN) Go down and shut the door, Carmen.

CHIEF OF POLICE: My tomb!

(CARMEN *goes out. A fairly long silence between* IRMA *and the* CHIEF OF POLICE, *who are now alone.*)

IRMA: I rang just now. I wanted to be alone with you for a moment.

(*A silence, during which they look each other gravely in the eyes.*) Tell me, George . . . (*She hesitates.*)

CHIEF OF POLICE: (*Slightly irritated*) Go on.

IRMA: How long are you going to carry on playing this game? No, don't look like that. Aren't you tired of it?

CHIEF OF POLICE: What do you mean? I shall be going home soon . . .

IRMA: If you can. If the revolution lets you.

CHIEF OF POLICE: Irma, you're mad, or you're pretending you are. The revolution's a game too. You can't see it from here, but every rebel is playing a game. And he likes his game.

IRMA: But what if they get carried away by the game? I mean, if they get so involved that they destroy everything and replace everything. Oh yes, I know, there's always the phoney detail which reminds them that at a certain moment and at a certain point in the drama they're supposed to stop, perhaps even withdraw . . . But if they get so carried away by their emotions that they don't realize what they're doing, and jump blindly into . . .

CHIEF OF POLICE: Reality? Is that what you want to say? So what? Let them try. I'll do the same – I'll penetrate whichever level of reality the game is being played on, and as I've got the best part, I shall win.

IRMA: They'll be stronger than you.

CHIEF OF POLICE: Rubbish! Look at the resources I've got, the treasure. My bodyguard's downstairs. I'm in constant liaison with all my departments. Anyway, that's enough of that. Are you or are you not mistress of a House of Illusions? You are. Right. If I come to see you it's to satisfy myself in your mirrors, and in their tricks. (*Tenderly*) Don't worry. Everything will be the same as it always has been.

IRMA: I don't know why, but I *am* worried today. Carmen seems strange. The rebels – how shall I put it – have a sort of seriousness about them . . .

CHIEF OF POLICE: Their role demands it.

IRMA: No no . . . a sort of determination. The ones I see going by the windows look threatening, but they're not singing. The threat is in their eyes.

CHIEF OF POLICE: So what? Suppose it is – do you think I'm a coward? Do you think I ought to give up and go home?

IRMA: (*Thoughtfully*) No. And anyway, I think it's too late. Let's talk about something else.

CHIEF OF POLICE: (*Extremely irritated*) If you wish.

IRMA: Let's talk about us.

CHIEF OF POLICE: Here we go again. I suppose you're going to bring up our great love story.

IRMA: No, not our love story, but the time when we used to love one another.

CHIEF OF POLICE: Come on, then. Let's have it! Recite its history! Sing its praises! I suppose you think my visits would be less savoury if you didn't flavour them with the remembrance of an alleged innocence.

IRMA: It's a question of tenderness. Neither the most extravagant inventions of my customers, nor my wealth, nor all the effort I put into finding new themes for my studios, nor the passing of time, nor the carpets, nor the gilding, nor the crystals, nor the cold, can prevent there having been moments when you forgot yourself in my arms, or prevent me from remembering them.

CHIEF OF POLICE: Do you regret those moments?

IRMA: (*Tenderly*) I'd give my whole kingdom to relive a single one of them! And you know which one. All I need is one single word of truth – like when you look at your wrinkles at night, or when you're cleaning your teeth.

CHIEF OF POLICE: It's too late. (*Pause.*) We couldn't lose

45

ourselves in one another for ever. Anyway, you don't know the direction I was already secretly moving in when I was in your arms.

IRMA: I know that I loved you . . .

CHIEF OF POLICE: Could you do without Arthur?

IRMA: (*Laughing nervously*) But it was you who forced him on me. You insisted on there being a man in the house – against my wishes and against my better judgement – a man in this domain, which should have remained virginal . . . Idiot, don't laugh. Virginal. In other words, sterile. But you wanted there to be a pillar, a shaft, a phallus on the premises, standing stiff and erect. So we've got one. You saddled me with that lump of congested meat, that blushing violet with the arms of a wrestler. He may look like the strong man at the fair, but you've no idea how feeble he really is. You stupidly forced him on me, because you felt you were getting old.

CHIEF OF POLICE: Shut up!

IRMA: You were so busy with power. But even that wasn't enough for you. So you started coming back here again and amused yourself, watching Arthur as your go-between.

CHIEF OF POLICE: The situation has become dangerous again, so I'm not bored, and I've lost my taste for pleasure by proxy. Through action I've become active again, and I want you. Throw Arthur out.

IRMA: I'm his man, he relies on me. Anyway, I need that stupid, musclebound phoney hanging on to my apron strings. He's my body, if you like, set beside me.

CHIEF OF POLICE: I'm jealous!

IRMA: Jealous of that great big doll who makes up as a torturer to satisfy a straw judge? Listen, darling, you didn't always object when I appeared to you under the appearance of that magnificent body . . .

CHIEF OF POLICE: Shut up.

IRMA: No; I feel like talking. Catastrophe is staring me in the face. I had a dream last night, a premonition . . .

CHIEF OF POLICE: Tell me.

IRMA: I can't. I'm afraid!

CHIEF OF POLICE: The police are guarding the house, for Christ's sake.

46

IRMA: (*Shrugging her shoulders*) And who's guarding the police? I feel like talking because in this tense situation it's the only way I can share your pathos. To start with, so as to see things clearly, I want to go back to our first night . . .

CHIEF OF POLICE: (*Slaps* IRMA's *face: she falls on to the divan.*) Cut it out. And don't cry, or I'll smash your face in. If I ever hear that you've been telling people what happened I'll send your whorehouse up in smoke. I'll set fire to your hair and your bush, and turn you loose. I'll light up the whole town with blazing whores. (*Very gently*) Do you believe I'm capable of it?

IRMA: (*In a whisper*) Yes, darling.

CHIEF OF POLICE: Right, then – let's have your accounts. You can deduct Apollo's crêpe de chine, if you like. And hurry up about it, I've got to get back to my post. For the time being, I've got to act . . . After that, things will run themselves. My name will act in my place. Any news?

IRMA: From Chantal, before she deserted us. The power-station will be occupied at about 3 a.m.

CHIEF OF POLICE: Are you sure? Who told her?

IRMA: The partisans of the fourth sector.

CHIEF OF POLICE: Could be. I can imagine how she found out!

IRMA: She was the only one who used to tell tales – the only one. Don't you start running down my house . . .

CHIEF OF POLICE: Your brothel, my love.

IRMA: Brothel. Bawdy house. Bagnio. Knocking shop. Fuckery. Whore-house. Call it what you like. Chantal's the only one who's on the other side. She's deserted. But before she went, she took Carmen into her confidence, and Carmen's no fool.

CHIEF OF POLICE: Who was her contact?

IRMA: Roger. The plumber. It's a stupid story. It isn't easy for men to get in here: it's a convent. By men, I mean . . .

CHIEF OF POLICE: The ones who keep their heads?

IRMA: Nicely put. Well, I said he could come and see to the plumbing. It costs me a fortune every month . . . Are you interested, by the way?

CHIEF OF POLICE: In your plumbing? I'll send you my Head of Department.

IRMA: Thanks. Anyway: I let the plumber come. What d'you

47

imagine he looks like? Young and handsome? Not at all. Forty, Thick-set. Serious, ironic-looking. Chantal used to talk to him. I turned him out. Too late. He belonged to the Andromeda network.

CHIEF OF POLICE: Andromeda? Bravo. The revolution is giving itself airs, it's getting above itself. If it calls its sectors after the constellations, it'll soon evaporate and be metamorphosed into song. Let's hope they're nice songs.

IRMA: Suppose their songs give the revolutionaries courage? Suppose they're prepared to die for them?

CHIEF OF POLICE: The sweetness of their songs will make them go soft. Unfortunately, they haven't got to the point of softness or sweetness yet. In any case, Chantal's amours were providential.

IRMA: Don't bring God into this.

CHIEF OF POLICE: I'm a freemason. So . . .

IRMA: *You* are? You never told me.

CHIEF OF POLICE: (*Solemnly*) Sublime Prince of the Royal Secret!

IRMA: (*Amused*) You, a masonic brother! In a little apron! With a little mallet, and a hood, and a taper! That's really funny. (*Pause.*) You too?

CHIEF OF POLICE: What d'you mean? You too?

IRMA: (*With mock solemnity*) Behold the Guardian of Infinitely More Solemn Rites!
(*They both laugh for a long time.*)

CHIEF OF POLICE: What about Arthur, then?

IRMA: He'll be dead this evening.

CHIEF OF POLICE: Dead? You mean . . . really dead?

IRMA: Oh, come on, George . . . the way people die here.

CHIEF OF POLICE: Ah! . . . Who's it for?

IRMA: The minister . . .

CARMEN: (*Coming back, out of breath*) Madam, there are three men downstairs . . .

IRMA: What d'you mean? There wasn't anyone there. I rang.

CARMEN: There was. They'd just come in. They were at the bottom of the stairs, three young men.

IRMA: If they're under age, don't let them up.

CHIEF OF POLICE: Who are they? Soldiers?

CARMEN: They didn't say a word to me (*To* IRMA) I think it's you they've come to see.

IRMA: Me? But what are they like?

CARMEN: (*Searching for her words*) They're beautiful! Beautiful – but like you see in dreams . . .

IRMA: (*Almost shouting*) My dream!

CHIEF OF POLICE: I asked you to tell it to me . . .

IRMA: I can't.

CHIEF OF POLICE: You can try.

IRMA: I wasn't actually asleep, but I was terribly tired, and I was dozing in an armchair. The atmosphere was very heavy. The air was humid. I was melting. At one moment even, I thought I was going to turn into a tiny pool of warm water which someone would come and find under the chair. I could hear bursts of machine-gun fire in the distance. It might have been to escape from the fire that I saw myself a pool of liquid . . . All of a sudden I heard music (*Music is heard.*) . . . as if the clouds were being torn apart (*The lace hangings above them suddenly tear.*) . . .

CARMEN: (*Calling out*) Studio Seventeen, still known as the Hall of Dreams! (*She claps her hands.*) Bring the studio down, Elyane, hurry! Into the studio, gentlemen. (*She claps her hands again.*) Come on, gentlemen . . .

(*The stage blacks out at this moment, but lights come on in the chandeliers. After each different bit of music, we hear:*)

> Blood!
> Tears!
> Sperm!

(*The three protagonists have disappeared. Three very beautiful* YOUNG MEN *seem to be descending from the flies: they are the* YOUNG MEN *we saw on the stairs in scene 5. They personify* BLOOD, TEARS *and* SPERM. *All three are wounded.*)

BLOOD: Shall we speak, or . . .

TEARS: Banal words, or strange moods? Who are we? Where are we? If our fathers – the gods – are rivers circulating in men, we have overflowed. Ours is a strange adventure. Shall I remind you of it? Brothers – who are only myself. Were we at first just three words emblazoned by poets on the backcloth of night –

and was it our longing to escape from that that gave us the appearance we have today . . .

BLOOD: . . . or, swimming against the tide of veins and vessels, did we come here from an immortal source to explore these three mysterious words? And should our appearance vanish behind them? I've been waiting for a long time to escape from the word, so as to be able to use it . . .

TEARS: Our beautiful names condemn us to Night – which is close to Death. We shall find it difficult to get over that, and start *using* language.

SPERM: Like you, like death, I feel I'm a prisoner of a long period of decorative misuse . . .

IRMA: (*Coming in slowly, as if pushed against her will. She is holding a pair of scissors and a roll of gauze.*) I haven't done anything. And I can't see why you're pursuing me . . . here, in my house . . .

TEARS: Are you so surprised that we decided – or that the gods led us – to appear to you here?

IRMA: I'm tired – I'm asleep.

SPERM: It's sleep we haunt, or daydreams. Don't be surprised. After all, we don't wish you harm. Nor good, either.

IRMA: I have nothing to do with you! I don't know who you are!

BLOOD: We are all three of us wounded, and we thought that we'd be best looked after, here, in this house. You have everything . . . bandages . . . Hurry up.

IRMA: There's no iodine or antiseptic, and my hands are dirty. My house is empty. Except for the costumes and masks.

SPERM: (*Interrupting her*) Don't say anything against masks. You owe everything beautiful on earth to masks.

IRMA: And everything good?

TEARS: We're wounded. Hurry up.

IRMA: (*In a panic*) You're mad! You must be three criminals, no one heard you come in. Go away, then! Get out! Go away! Get out of here!

BLOOD: Madam, we never stop flowing. Torrents, rivers, basins, torrential rains, cataracts, geysers that we exhaust ourselves to fill, and whose source . . .

IRMA: (*In a panic*) . . . is hidden, like that of the Nile, and multiple . . . Go away! Criminals, go away, get out!

TEARS: (*Very sadly*) The image I now invest you with is heartbreaking, if the face of a man crucified . . .

IRMA: (*Suddenly solemn*) Be quiet! Go away! If you don't leave, gentlemen, I shall wake up.

(*The three* YOUNG MEN *are puzzled. Suddenly* MADAM IRMA *stoops, cuts off a piece of gauze and winds it round the naked thigh of one of the* YOUNG MEN. *Gradual blackout. When the lights come up again,* IRMA *and the* CHIEF OF POLICE *are in their previous places.*)

IRMA: (*Calling out*) Lock up Studio 17! Hurry up, Elyane. And pull the studio up . . .

(*There is a sudden knock at the door.*)

No no, wait a minute. . . .

(*The door opens and* ARTHUR *appears. He is trembling and his clothes are torn.*)

(*Throwing herself into his arms*) Darling! What is it! Are you wounded? . . . Say something!

ARTHUR: (*Panting*) I tried to get through to police headquarters. (*To the* CHIEF OF POLICE) Looking for you! Impossible! The whole town's ablaze. The rebels are in control almost everywhere. I don't know how you managed to get here, Chief, but you'll never get back. I finally managed to get through to the Royal Palace. I saw the Grand Chamberlain. He said he'd try to come. He even shook my hand, by the way. Then I left.

(*Enter* CARMEN.)

CARMEN: Madam, the Grand Chamberlain's here. The Queen's envoy.

ARTHUR: The women are the most excited. They're urging the men on to loot and kill. But the most terrible thing was a girl singing a song . . .

(*There is a shot. A windowpane is shattered. So is the mirror, near the bed.* ARTHUR *falls, hit in the forehead by a bullet from outside.*)

CHIEF OF POLICE: So I'm stuck here? In a brothel! I'll have to make it my headquarters.

IRMA: (*Bitterly*) I've still got my jewels, my diamonds . . . perhaps . . .

CARMEN: (*Softly*) If the house is going to be blown up . . . Is the Saint Theresa costume in the wardrobe, Madam Irma?

IRMA: On the left. Get them to take Arthur away first. I'm going to receive the Envoy.

(*The stage moves from left to right, as before, but between this scene and the next there is a fairly long space of time in which the darkness is broken up by flashes, bursts of machine-gun fire, vague cries and sighs.*)

SCENE 7

The interior of a café, 1900 style. Mirrors. Bottles on shelves. Counter.
At the back, ROGER, *forty, a typical proletarian leader, is writing at a little table without looking up.* ARMAND, *twenty-five, silent, is sitting on a banquette.* MARC, *standing up holding a map, is moving little flags according to the directives he receives over the phone.*
Downstage, CHANTAL *is just finishing bandaging the arm of a wounded rebel. She hesitates over where to put the pin.* GEORGETTE, *about thirty, nervous, snatches the pin out of her hand and fixes it himself.* LUC, *thirty, is sitting in silence.*

GEORGETTE: Your eyes finger everything you do.

CHANTAL: I've got to look where to put the pin.

GEORGETTE: You don't look, you ogle.

WOUNDED MAN: What's happening outside?

GEORGETTE: The sectors are joining up. We'll win.

WOUNDED MAN: Is there a real hope?

GEORGETTE: No. To hope is to dream. We'll win.

WOUNDED MAN: But what about the Archbishop . . .? And the General . . .? And the Judge?

GEORGETTE: We're fighting men. When their men start losing, the Great Figures crumble.

ROGER: How long are you going to stand there primping?

ARMAND: I'm arranging my hardware for the ball.

ROGER: Not the ball, the fight.

ARMAND: The fight then. Bang, bang, bang, etc.

ROGER: It's not a game!

ARMAND: Why not? Bang, bang, bang, etc.

ROGER: It's work.

ARMAND: It's a lot better than work. Bang, bang, etc.

ROGER: Shut up.

52

ARMAND: Why the hell can't we play? The other side do.

ROGER: The day we get pleasure out of shooting men, or anything else, it'll be goodbye to the revolutionary spirit.

ARMAND: All week long we operate machines, and on a great day like this, instead of raising hell, we fiddle.

ROGER: The law courts have been burned to the ground. The churches have been looted. Men going out to fight in judges' robes and surplices. It's a bloody carnival. What more do you want?

ARMAND: Our carnivals are always a mockery of theirs.

ROGER: Later on, we'll organize leisure activities . . .

WOUNDED MAN: Take it easy! You're not washing a corpse. For Christ's sake, take it easy.

CHANTAL: Oh, shut up, it's only iodine.

GEORGETTE: Being rough is also a game.

CHANTAL: 'The main thing is to look after the wounded.'

GEORGETTE: The main thing is not to play games.

ROGER: Exactly. The revolution should begin by despising make-believe.

CHANTAL: Like the make-believe that I have a talent for dressing wounds?

LOUIS: Right.

(LUKE *enters*.)

ROGER: Listen. The other side plays. What we're engaged in is more serious. If we behave like the other side, then we *are* the other side. Instead of changing the world, all we'll achieve is a reflection of the one we want to destroy.

GEORGETTE: Everything must be aimed at utility.

ROGER: It's better to remain silent and motionless than to say or do anything that can't be utilized . . .

GEORGETTE: . . . for the revolution.

ARMAND: In a minute, I'm going for a pee. That's a utility. It's also a necessity. At the same time, you mean I can't amuse myself by squirting it up along the wall?

ROGER: You mean you play childish games like that during a revolution!

ARMAND: Then what can I do?

ROGER: The people mustn't amuse themselves, and they mustn't play. From now on they've got to be in dead earnest.

LOUIS: In certain cases, you've got to use the enemies' weapons.

LUKE: Provided we storm the barricades, what does it matter if we do it in the name of freedom or in the name of Chantal?

ROGER: Men don't revolt in order to go chasing after a female.

LUKE: Even if the chase leads them to victory?

ROGER: Then their victory is already sick. It's got the clap. What do you want, anyway?

LUKE: Chantal.

ROGER: Chantal! Why?

LUKE: We need someone to spur on our section.

ROGER: Try courage.

LUKE: We need Chantal to sing. To work them up.

ROGER: Buy a bugle.

ARMAND: Or a bazooka!

ROGER: That's all you ever talk about, bazookas. Bazookas, bazookas. Like some sort of talisman. No bazookas!

ARMAND: How are we supposed to fight, then – hand to hand?

ROGER: Yes, it eliminates distance.

LUKE: Why do you distrust enthusiasm?

ROGER: I distrust emotionalism. It's like a carnival outside. People like him are shooting for the fun of it.

ARMAND: And why not? It's real, it's exciting! Gun in one hand, cock in the other. Shoot and screw! Shoot and screw!

ROGER: Don't talk like that. That's not what it's about! Who do you think you are.

ARMAND: The darling of the gods.

ROGER: No, not the gods. If the heavens are studded with constellations like the archbishops, then we've got to tear heaven down. Not invoke it, not even name it, but strip it, and make it dance naked on the cathedral squares.

LOUIS: We've got to take advantage of youthful enthusiasm. The young can't fight without war cries. They only get wounded to show their scars.

LUKE: Lend us Chantal.

ROGER: No. Chantal was useful at the beginning of the revolution. She's played her part. Now she's got to nurse.

CHANTAL: Which I can't.

ROGER: Which you must.

LUKE: Lend us Chantal.

ROGER: No! (*With sudden anger*) What the hell do you want? I didn't pull Chantal out of one brothel to put her into another – even if it is a mockery of the first. Carnival! Carnival! You know as well as I do that a carnival that goes to the limit is suicide.

LUKE: Without the people's anger, there'd be no revolt. And anger is a carnival.

ROGER: Then we must fight without anger. Reason should be enough.

LOUIS: You're dreaming.

ROGER: What?

CHANTAL: I want to sing! To sing the excitement of the brawl. That's all, just sing, for justice, for the fighters for justice.

ROGER: That's over, Chantal. You promised!

CHANTAL: I know, but I can't nurse. I'm sorry, Roger, I'm no good at it. All I can do is sing. All I want to do is sing.

ROGER: But you can't give up now. You were my first convert. I began with you.

WOUNDED MAN: Is that you, Chantal? I didn't recognize you! What the hell are you doing here instead of leading the men forward like you did yesterday, on the parapet? (*A silence.*) It takes women like you to loosen us up. It's your voice that tears up the cobblestones. It's your voice that stretches the barbed wire. It's your voice . . .

LUKE: Let us have her for two hours.

ROGER: Chantal belongs to me.

LUKE: To the insurrection.

CHANTAL: To nobody.

ROGER: To my section – to me. If you want a woman to lead men forward, then create one.

LUKE: We tried to. We looked for one. We tried to build one up: nice voice, nice breasts, with the right kind of manner, but . . . her eyes lacked fire . . . we asked the north quarter, and the port quarter, to let us have theirs; they weren't free.

CHANTAL: A woman like me? Another one? You mean I have two popular rivals – two other poor devils? Let them come. I'll wipe the floor with them. I have no rival.

ROGER: Chantal, please!

LUKE: She'll hardly have anything to do. We're attacking the bridge at dawn. She'll sing from the balcony.

ROGER: If I lend her to you.

LUKE: If we take her, we'll hire her.

CHANTAL: How much?

ROGER: You think that's funny! Supposing she got killed, we'd lose everything, she's irreplaceable.

LUKE: How many women do you want in exchange – ten – twenty?

CHANTAL: Is that all?

ROGER: Chantal!

(*Suddenly a terrible explosion. The windowpanes rattle. The four men pull themselves together. They look at each other anxiously. The phone rings.*)

MARK: Yes – B88O – yes – eh? – who? – Good – yes! (*He hangs up.*) They've blown up the palace.

ROGER: You won't need Chantal.

MARK: The tribunal's already in session.

LUKE: Executions?

MARK: Immediately upon condemnation.

(*Enter* ARMAND, *in a state of wild excitement.*)

ARMAND: The palace has been blown up! You can see it blazing from the windows! Everything's giving way.

ROGER: What about the Queen and the Archbishop, and the others?

ARMAND: Dead, I suppose.

LUKE: And if not?

ROGER: Undress them!

ARMAND: But they're sacred – I mean, I don't think so, but – what do we replace them with?

MARK: Ourselves and Chantal.

ROGER: Why Chantal?

MARK: We must counter their carnival with our own.

ROGER: Carnival?

MARK: We must use Chantal. Her job's to embody the revolution. The job of our heroes is to die with a smile. The job of the mothers and widows is to mourn the dead. The job of the dead is to cry for revenge. Chantal will rouse the people and sing. Chantal embodies the struggle . . . the people are waiting for Chantal to represent victory.

CHANTAL: What, me? With my raucous voice, my phoney anger, my drugged eyes, my painted face, my Andalusian hair. Me, embody the struggle? And win? What sort of a victory will

56

that be?

ROGER: And what will we gain?

MARK: There'll be time to think about that later.

CHANTAL: The face of an inspired owl and a hoarse voice, that I give or lend for hate. All I am is my face, my voice, and inside me the sweet poison of kindness.

ROGER: I love you, Chantal.

LOUIS: What you love in Chantal is the very thing you're bent on destroying, the thing that made it possible for her to enter the brothel, the thing that's still part of her.

MARK: And because it's still part of her, she'll electrify the people. We must invent a Chantal who becomes more and more fabulous! Loudspeakers everywhere. Her voice at all the barricades. Photos. Her face on all the hoardings. Print leaflets, thousands of them – get them distributed. Bright colours. With a picture of her and a declaration. Invent a historic slogan signed Chantal. Write a poem to the glory of anger, revolution, war.

ROGER: Hailing freedom, the people, their virtue.

MARK: Christ, no! Bump them up into a heaven of abstractions and you'll never get them down again. Magnify freedom, the people, virtue, and you'll make them untouchable. Leave them in their living reality. Let there be poems and pictures, excitement, even ecstasy, but not of pleasure – only pain.

(*Exit* MARK, LUKE, WOUNDED MAN, ARMAND, CHANTAL.)

LOUIS: You're dreaming. Dreaming of an impossible revolution, carried out reasonably, unemotionally. You're fascinated by it, the way the other side is by other games . . . But you've got to realize that when he pulls a trigger the most reasonable man always manages to become a self-appointed judge.

ROGER: In whose eyes?

(LOUIS *shrugs and exits. Exit* ROGER *and* GEORGETTE *in different directions.*)

SCENE 8

The Funeral Parlour, which MADAM IRMA *referred to when she was enumerating her rooms. This room is in ruins. The black lace and velvet*

57

hangings are in shreds. An impression of devastation. Irma's dress is in rags. So is the Chief of Police's uniform. Arthur's corpse is on a kind of false tomb of false black marble. Near it, a new character: the COURT ENVOY. *Dressed as an ambassador, he is the only one in good shape.* CARMEN *is dressed as she was at the beginning. There is a formidable explosion. Everything shakes.*

ENVOY: (*Both casual and serious*) For more centuries than I care to name, the centuries have been wearing themselves away refining me, subtilizing me . . . (*He smiles.*) I don't know quite what it was about that explosion – the combination perhaps of power with the tinkle of jewellery and broken mirrors – but something tells me that it was the royal palace . . . (*They all exchange horror-stricken glances.*) Let us show no emotion. Provided we are not like that . . . (*He points to* ARTHUR's *corpse.*)

IRMA: (*Touching the corpse with her foot*) He never thought he'd be playing his corpse part this evening without having to.

ENVOY: (*Smiling*) Our dear Home Secretary would have been delighted – had he not suffered the same fate. It is I, unfortunately, who have had to replace him in this mission to you, and I have no taste for pleasure of this kind.
(*He pinches* CARMEN's *chin. She is wearing the Saint Theresa costume.*)
We prefer this modest rose. I'm very pleased with her. Everything went off admirably – to our great satisfaction. (*Suddenly embarrassed*) Despite the apparent irritation of the fair lady.

CARMEN: (*Dryly*) I did my job.

IRMA: (*To* CARMEN) Be quiet. (*To the* ENVOY) Forgive her, your Excellency, she feels she's come down in the world because with you she's only a saint. She enjoyed a higher rank with one of the other gentlemen. But she knows her duty.

ENVOY: Then it is for me to apologize. (*He touches* ARTHUR's *corpse with his foot.*) Yes, this corpse would have sent our dear Minister into raptures.

IRMA: Don't you believe it, your Excellency. What such gentlemen want is illusion. The minister wanted a make-believe corpse. And Arthur is a real one. Look at him: he looks much more alive, now he's dead. Everything in him was hastening towards immobility.

ENVOY: He was made for grandeur, then.

CHIEF OF POLICE: What, him? That flabby, overblown . . .

ENVOY: He, like us, was tormented by the quest for immobility. By what we call the hieratic. And in passing, allow me to salute the imagination responsible for including a funeral parlour in this house.

IRMA: (*Proudly*) You haven't seen the half of it.

ENVOY: Whose idea was it?

IRMA: The wisdom of nations, your Excellency.

ENVOY: It does well. But let us return to the Queen . . .

CHIEF OF POLICE: Yes! Where is she?

ENVOY: (*Lightly*) She's embroidering. For a moment she thought of nursing the wounded. But she was persuaded that, since the throne was threatened, she ought to insist on the extreme observance of the royal prerogative.

IRMA: Which is?

ENVOY: Absence. Her Majesty has retired to one of her apartments in solitude. She is saddened by the disobedience of her people. She is embroidering a handkerchief. This is the design: the four corners will be embellished with poppy heads. In the middle of the handkerchief, embroidered in pale blue silk, there will be a swan, motionless upon the water. It is here that her Majesty becomes a little uneasy: shall the water be that of a lake, or a pond, or a pool? Or simply of a tank, or a cup? This a serious problem. We have chosen it because it is insoluble, and because the Queen may well withdraw into infinite meditation.

IRMA: Is the Queen amused?

ENVOY: Her Majesty, too, is rapidly moving towards immobility.

IRMA: And she's embroidering?

ENVOY: No, Madam. I say that the Queen is embroidering a handkerchief, for although it is my duty to describe her, it is also my duty to conceal her.

IRMA: Do you mean she's not embroidering?

ENVOY: I mean that the Queen is embroidering, and that she isn't embroidering. She picks her nose, examines the snot extirpated, and then lies down. After which she dries the dishes.

IRMA: The Queen does?

ENVOY: No. A woman does. All women do that.

IRMA: But the Queen?

ENVOY: She is not nursing the wounded. She is embroidering an invisible handkerchief . . .

CHIEF OF POLICE: For Christ's sake! What have you done with her Majesty? And stop going round in circles.

ENVOY: She's in a coffer. She's asleep. Wrapped in the recesses of royalty, she snores . . .

CHIEF OF POLICE: (*Threateningly*) Is the Queen dead?

ENVOY: (*Impassively*) She snores – and she doesn't snore. Her tiny head bears, unbowed, a crown of metal and stones.

CHIEF OF POLICE: (*More and more threateningly*) All right, all right! The Queen's in danger. So what can we do? I still have practically the whole police force behind me. They're ready to die for me . . . They know who I am, and what I'll do for them . . . I've got a part to play too, remember. But if the Queen is dead – then it's different. I need her, it's in her name that I'm working towards my own. What's the present state of the revolution? In plain language.

ENVOY: All is lost – it seems.

IRMA: You are a man of the Court, your Excellency. I'm a woman of the people. Before I came here I was with the troops – my baptism of fire, so to speak – and I can assure you I've been in far worse situations than this. I fought to get away from the people, and now they're back, howling beneath my windows, I'll fight again! My house still stands. My rooms aren't intact, but they're still there. My whores – except for one lunatic – are still on the job. If the kingpin of the palace is a woman like me . . .

ENVOY: (*Imperturbably*) The Queen is standing on one leg in the middle of an empty room, and she . . .

CHIEF OF POLICE: Stop it! I'm fed up with your riddles. The Queen, for me, has to be someone. And the situation has to be concrete! Describe it exactly as it is. Come on!

ENVOY: What do you want to save?

CHIEF OF POLICE: The Queen!

CARMEN: The flag!

IRMA: My skin!

ENVOY: (*To* CHIEF OF POLICE) If you're so determined to save the Queen – and beyond her, our flag, with its gilded fringe, its ropes and staff – would you care to tell me what they mean?

CHIEF OF POLICE: No! So far, I have served all those things admirably without ever bothering to know more about them than met my eye. I shall continue to do so. What's the present state of the revolution?

ENVOY: (*Resigned*) The park gates will be strong enough to keep the crowd out for a time. The guards are as loyal as we: it's a strange loyalty. They are ready to die for their sovereign. They will give their blood, but alas! there will not be enough to drown the revolution. There are piles of sandbags in front of the doors. And, so that even reason shall be confused, her Majesty keeps moving from one secret room to another, from the servants' hall to the throne room, from the latrines to the henhouse, to the chapel, to the guardroom . . . She makes it impossible to find her, and thus attains her threatened invisibility. So much for the interior of the palace. Outside, the people are so intoxicated by their first victories that they would happily exchange useful combat for useless sacrifice. There's no great difference after all. The people aren't really going into battle – they are taking part in a carnival.

IRMA: In a carnival, you've no idea what you're doing. You can be laughing so much that you get hold of a live wire . . .

ENVOY: Precisely. And you're not the only one who's realized. A revolutionary committee has been set up. You don't know much about it, but we have our spies everywhere.

CHIEF OF POLICE: So have I!

ENVOY: And I can assure you that it's becoming more and more of a threat. Its members are grim technicians. Dressed in black . . .

IRMA: Like in Studio 28.

ENVOY: (*Interrupting her*) Far from it. These fellows – and this seems to be a new angle – are not playing. Or rather, they don't realize what they're playing. They calculate. Their faces are pale and sad. They say precisely what they mean. They don't cheat. They have tremendous power over the people. They want to save them.

IRMA: Why don't we lure them into my studios . . .

CARMEN: Oh yes!

ENVOY: They've thought of that.

CHIEF OF POLICE: What about our side? What about the Commander in Chief?

ENVOY: Gone mad.

CHIEF OF POLICE: And the Attorney General?

ENVOY: Died of fright.

CHIEF OF POLICE: And the Bishop?

ENVOY: A more difficult case. The Church is discreet. Nothing definite is known. There was a rumour that his severed head had been seen on the handlebars of a bicycle, but naturally it was false. So you're the only one left. The only one we can rely on. And your orders aren't getting through . . .

CHIEF OF POLICE: Downstairs, in the corridors and studios, I have enough loyal men to protect us all . . .

ENVOY: (*Interrupting him*) In uniform?

CHIEF OF POLICE: Of course they're in uniform! They're my bodyguard. Can you imagine me with a bodyguard in sports jackets? In uniform. Black uniforms. With my armbands!

IRMA: Armbands?

CHIEF OF POLICE: Well, they're in their pockets for the moment. They're a fine body of men! With the will to win!

ENVOY: To win what? (*Pause.*) Would it worry you to look at the world calmly? To see things as they are? To accept responsibility for what you see?

CHIEF OF POLICE: Why did you come here, actually?

ENVOY: To save the Queen. The Quee-een. For my eyes refuse to perceive anything but appearances. They are resigned to them.

CHIEF OF POLICE: You came to see me, so you must have had something definite in mind. Have you got a plan?

ENVOY: (*After a silence*) Yes, Chief. But it is philosophical ideas that concern me at the moment.

IRMA: Tell us.

ENVOY: (*After a short period of meditation, and as if giving a lecture*) Ladies and Gentlemen. From my earliest youth, I was involved with the Court. My father, as you know, was the Lord Chamberlain. My mother was his wife, the princess, the daughter of a lord duke who was Lord Master of the Horse. (*The* CHIEF OF POLICE *and* IRMA *bow.*) You bow to my presence, but your bow is not addressed to my person. I am

62

sure of that, which is why I accept it . . . (*Thinks*) Perhaps, I am not so sure as I say I am. Let us say I am familiar with the Court, then. I remain involved in its splendours, and all the more attached to them when they are defaced and stained with blood. With what blood? Whether stains or noble haemorrhages, these blemishes point to tragedy. I relish tragedy. It enables us to depart more quickly from the elementary data. Now, here we find ourselves in the midst of the heroic struggle. If, as it would seem, we are all moving towards death, we actually go even further. I mean that our reason offers us, the living, the image of what we shall be in death; that is, in men's consciousnesses. We have only one preoccupation: that of suggesting a definitive statue to posterity, whether it be absurd or familiar, tender or severe, lovable or brutal, but one that should be perpetually impressive: eternal. Alas, our living eyes will never succeed in seeing ourselves in real death, nor our dead eyes in seeing ourselves in future consciousness, so we have therefore invented and perfected the elegant feat of fixing ourselves in life according to eternal attitudes. Is that clear?

IRMA: No!

ENVOY: When her Majesty . . . I beg your pardon, when you, Madam, pour the tea, with your elbow so, and your little finger . . . No, I beg your pardon . . . One of my comrades in arms – he was low-born – worked for a long time, day and night, to become an officer so that, if war broke out, death should strike him down in his officer's uniform and that, on the war memorial of his native village, his rank should be inscribed opposite his name. Got it?

CHIEF OF POLICE: Wait a minute . . . To become an officer, you say, you have to work day and night, and this work may lead to . . .?

ENVOY: What the work might lead to didn't interest him. Or interested him less, shall we say, than the image with which he aspired to be identified.

IRMA: When I pour the tea out, it's so's you can drink it.

ENVOY: It is 'so's I can drink it'. But it is also so that you can pour it for me. I beg your pardon: it's so that you shall have poured it for me – the Queen is embroidering and she is not

63

embroidering . . . If she sneezes, I know that her Majesty is there, in a sneeze, but in a sneeze that becomes sacred because it is the issue of – no no, Madam, not the issue of a person who has chosen to be Queen . . . (*Pause.*) Although . . .? But of her whom, perhaps a little carelessly, I have named Queen – so that that person who is constantly retreating, should make my own person constantly retreat in my own eyes, and precipitate me . . .

(*There is a sudden tremendous explosion. Both men, but not* IRMA *and* CARMEN, *throw themselves to the ground, then get up and dust each other off.*)

ENVOY: That could have been the Royal Palace. The Royal Palace is dead. Long live the Royal Palace!

IRMA: But earlier on . . . What about the other explosion . . .?

ENVOY: A royal palace never stops blowing up.

(CARMEN *throws a black sheet over* ARTHUR's *body, she tidies up a bit.*)

ENVOY: I must congratulate you, Madam, on your *sang-froid*. And on your courage . . . They merit the greatest respect . . . (*Thoughtfully*) The greatest . . .

IRMA: You're forgetting who you're talking to. I may keep a brothel, but I wasn't born of the union of the moon and a crocodile: I told you, I come from the people . . .

ENVOY: (*Harshly*) Forget the people. When life is ebbing, one's hands cling to a sheet. And what does that rag mean when you are about to penetrate into the fixity of Providence?

IRMA: You don't mean . . .?

ENVOY: (*Examining her in detail*) A superb animal! Sturdy thighs! Solid shoulders . . .!

IRMA: So I've been told. But if the Queen is dead . . .

ENVOY: (*Bowing*) Long live the Queen, Ma'am.

IRMA: (*First taken aback, and then irritated*) I don't like people taking the piss. Stop it. At once.

ENVOY: (*Eagerly*) The people, in their fury and their joy, are on the brink of ecstasy: it is for us to push them over.

IRMA: Instead of standing here talking rubbish, you'd better go and dig the Queen out. Even if she is slightly roasted . . .

ENVOY: (*Harshly*) No. A Queen stewed to a pulp is not presentable. And even when she was alive, she wasn't as beautiful as you.

IRMA: (*Looking at herself complacently in the mirror*) She was older, after all.

CHIEF OF POLICE: Just to get near her, just to be worthy of a single look from her – that's why we go to so much trouble. But if someone were She Herself . . .

(CARMEN *stops and listens.*)

IRMA: (*Suddenly very intimidated*) I've never learnt to talk properly. I'm always tongue-tied.

ENVOY: Everything has to take place in a silence which etiquette allows no one to break . . .

CHIEF OF POLICE: I'll get them to start clearing the ruins of the Royal Palace. If the Queen was shut up, as you said, in a coffer, we may be able to save her.

ENVOY: (*Shrugging his shoulders*) It was a rosewood coffer! So old, so worn . . .! (*To* IRMA, *running his hand over the back of her neck*) Yes, it needs solid vertebrae . . . they've got to carry quite a weight . . .

CHIEF OF POLICE: And what about me, eh? What about me? I'm the strong man in this country, yes, me! It's not Irma . . .

IRMA: (*To the* ENVOY) I'm not really a strong woman, your Excellency, I'm really very weak. I was only showing off just now . . .

ENVOY: (*Authoritatively*) We'll all help you. Around this delicate, precious kernel we shall forge a shell of gold and iron.

CHIEF OF POLICE: (*Furious*) What about me? Irma would come before me! All the effort I've put into making myself the boss will be wasted. She'll be living a life of luxury in her studios, and only having to nod her head . . . While I'm . . . bloody hell! I protest!

ENVOY: Don't forget that your image isn't represented in her studios yet.

IRMA: Let me think it over for –

ENVOY: A few seconds; there's no time to lose . . .

IRMA: (*In a pretentious voice*) There *was* some question in our old family archives of . . .

ENVOY: (*Harshly*) Nonsense, Madam Irma. We have genealogists working day and night for us in our vaults. History is their handmaiden. We haven't a minute to lose if we're going to crush the people, but – take heed! Their pathetic pride idolizes you, but it's quite capable of sacrificing you too. In their imagination you are red – with crimson robes, or blood. Your blood. If they kill their idols and throw them down the sewers, you'll be with them . . .

(*The same explosion is heard again. The* ENVOY *smiles.*)

CHIEF OF POLICE: It's an enormous risk.

CARMEN: (*Intervening*) That's for Madam Irma to decide. (*To* IRMA) The vestments are ready.

ENVOY: We must be quick. It's a race against the clock. Them or us. Think fast, Madam Irma.

IRMA: (*Her head in her hands*) I am, your Excellency, I am. I'm moving, as quickly as possible, towards my destiny . . . (*To* CARMEN) Carmen, where are the others? The Bishop, Judge and General?

CARMEN: Waiting to go home.

IRMA: What are they doing?

CARMEN: Looking at themselves in the mirrors.

IRMA: Get them ready – will you, Carmen, please?

CARMEN: My daughter is dead, Madam.

IRMA: Bravo, bravo. Your costume will help to persuade them. Tell them you come to them in the name of a superior truth.

ENVOY: (to CARMEN) And – what shall we make *you* into?

CARMEN: I am here for all eternity, Sir.

(*Exit* CARMEN.)

ENVOY: There's one other thing – and this is rather more delicate. I spoke of an image which for the last few days has been ascending the revolutionary heavens . . .

IRMA: Does the revolution have its heaven, too?

ENVOY: You needn't envy it. Chantal's image is circulating in the streets. It's an image that is both like, and unlike, her. It dominates the battles. At first the people were fighting against illustrious and illusory tyrants, then for liberty, and tomorrow they'll be prepared to die for Chantal.

IRMA: Ungrateful bitch! When she was in such demand as Nell Gwynn!

CHIEF OF POLICE: She won't last. She's like me – no father or mother. And if she becomes an image, we'll use it. (*Pause.*) . . . A mask . . .

ENVOY: You owe everything beautiful on earth to masks.

66

(*A bell suddenly rings.* IRMA *is about to hurry over to it, but she changes her mind.*)

IRMA: I've made up my mind. I imagine that I have been called throughout eternity, and that God will bless me. I shall go and prepare myself in prayer . . .

ENVOY: (*Gravely*) Have you the costumes?

IRMA: My wardrobes are as famous as my studios! (*To the* CHIEF OF POLICE) George . . . This is our last moment together! After this, it won't be us any more . . .

(*The* ENVOY *moves away from them discreetly and goes over to the window.*)

CHIEF OF POLICE: We'll see each other every day.

IRMA: You'll see the Queen, and I the Hero.

CHIEF OF POLICE: With us inside.

IRMA: No. We must reduce 'us' till we disappear. So that when we die, what will seem to die will be only a gilded corpse.

CHIEF OF POLICE: Then refuse – there's still time.

IRMA: But I'm doing it for you, George – for your simulacrum and your tomb.

CHIEF OF POLICE: I love you.

IRMA: In a few minutes the metamorphosis will begin. We'll be strangers to each other, for ever and ever. Well, George, shall we do it?

ENVOY: (*Sounding extremely detached*) Think about a plain in the northern part of the country – a vast plain. Near by, a mountain of marble – of red marble . . .

CHIEF OF POLICE: Marble! And granite – pink granite?

ENVOY: Pink granite! Perhaps even porphyry . . .

CHIEF OF POLICE: Porphyry!

ENVOY: I refer, of course, to the project for a tomb.

CHIEF OF POLICE: I knew it, I knew it! The plans – where are the plans? Show me the plans.

ENVOY: Later. Imagine a tremendous structure – five or six law courts piled one on top of the other, a dozen opera houses, twenty large railway stations, thirty pagodas, one hundred war memorials, and you'll have a slight idea of what it will be. On one mountain we shall pile another, and on that other yet another, and in the very middle of the first, a tiny sentry box made of diamonds . . .

CHIEF OF POLICE: And shall I be able to keep vigil in it – standing or sitting – for my entire death?

ENVOY: Whoever acquires it will be there, dead, for all eternity. The world will be organized around it. The planets and suns will revolve around it. It will be unquestionably the most imposing funeral pile in the universe. From a secret point in the third mountain a road will run, which, after many complications, will end in another secret point where mirrors will reflect to infinity – I say to infinity – the image . . .

CHIEF OF POLICE: I'll do it!

ENVOY: . . . of a dead man!

CHIEF OF POLICE: I'll do it, I'll do it, I'll do it!

IRMA: And I'll be real? My dress will be real? And all my lace, and my jewels, will be real? The rest of the world will be a copy of what I'll be?

(*Crackle of machine-gun fire.*)

ENVOY: (*After a last glance through the shutters*) Yes, but hurry. Go to your apartments. Embroider an interminable handkerchief . . . (*To the* CHIEF OF POLICE) And you – go and give your last orders to your last men.

(IRMA *exits*.)

CHIEF OF POLICE: There's just one thing, though.

ENVOY: Yes? (*Goes over to the mirror. Takes a whole collection of decorations out of his pocket and pins them on to his tunic.*)

CHIEF OF POLICE: The others . . . You know – the Bishop, the Judge and the General. What if, by appearing, and starting their ceremonies again in public, their gestures gradually lose their rigidity, their ritual varnish, and become supple enough to inscribe themselves in real life? In short, if they were to become a real Bishop, Judge and General . . .

ENVOY: (*Viciously*) Oh, get on with it! I'm fed up listening to your crap!

SCENE 9

Decor as in the first three scenes, with the GENERAL, *the* BISHOP *and the* JUDGE *all present. Enter* CARMEN. *The* GENERAL, *who had been lying down, stands up and gives* CARMEN *a military salute, which seems to satisfy her. They don't speak.*

BISHOP: Carmen, you know yourself it's madness! It was stupid of me to come back here to hide.

CARMEN: Do you love your Queen, Bishop?

BISHOP: What a question!

CARMEN: Well, I doubt it. You could have gone home last night. The streets were dangerous, yes, but with a little ingenuity you could have found your way back to your house, your wife, your son.

BISHOP: The rebels were blocking the streets. They were shooting from the roofs, from the cellars . . . Bullets in your head, bullets in your feet . . .

CARMEN: OK, Bishop. So you preferred to stay and take refuge here, at Irma's, knowing that this house was a target, and that you might die here. If I understand right, you wanted to go up in flames in the midst of everything you hold dear?

BISHOP: I forbid you to mention such things.

CARMEN: Oh, come off it. This isn't the moment for putting on an act – especially the delicacy bit. No one knows your charming little drama better than I do. Don't pretend to be shocked. Orders have come from on high that you are to be enthroned definitively in your role.

BISHOP: You're mad.

CARMEN: Anyway, you've got to put your vestments on. You're going to enter into the skin, the soul, the mind, and all the consequences of the Bishop. I insist on it being done perfectly. And for as long as I wish . . . (*Rings.*)

BISHOP: What! Flaunt my shame in public? Make a public fool of myself? I refuse – categorically refuse.

CARMEN: No one but us will know . . .

BISHOP: It'd be enough for me to know, for me to be aware of the imposture . . .

CARMEN: What imposture? How will you be more or less a bishop than anyone else, and here rather than there . . .?

BISHOP: But you have to have studied. Ordination, unction, and all that kind of thing. And I'm only a gasman. I'm only at ease with Rosine.

ROSINE: Here I am. Did you ring?

CARMEN: Yes . . . Uniform 17. And quickly.

69

(*Exit* ROSINE.)

She'll be there to help you to start with. How will you still be a gasman if no one recognizes you as a gasman? Because you can add up? So can a bishop! Anyway, you won't be adding up any more. You'll begin by knowing nothing. And afterwards, how can you not be a bishop if everyone recognizes you as a bishop? You see I didn't say that you'd be this bishop or that bishop. You'll be the Bishop – it's as simple as that.

(ROSINE *returns*.)

Idiot. I said the costume from Room 17. Look what you've got there.

ROSINE: Oh, I'm sorry, Miss Carmen . . . But with this war the uniforms are all mixed up. I don't know where I am.

CARMEN: The Bishop's costume. And be quick about it. (ROSINE *exits. To the* BISHOP) Your role will be easy. You will appear – but first you'll bow to the Queen . . .

BISHOP: Is she here?

CARMEN: You will bow to your sovereign. The General and you will pay homage to her. And you, Judge . . .

JUDGE: Never, I'll never be able to! I haven't studied law. I shan't be able to judge according to the statute book.

CARMEN: She'll accept it.

JUDGE: You're making me commit a crime . . .

CARMEN: A judge judges not according to the statute book, but according to the dignity of his office, and the inspiration of God. Then the Hero will appear. The Queen and he, with you on either side of them, will appear on the grand Balcony of this house.

JUDGE: My pride forbids me . . .

CARMEN: Every day you'll be given hundreds of thousands of guilty people. Think of that. You won't have to crawl to attain the dignity of a judge; I shall bring it to you. The air will ring with the acclamations of the crowd.

JUDGE: Do you listen at doors?

CARMEN: The whole world knows what goes on here. The Queen will bow.

JUDGE: Carmen!

CARMEN: The Hero will bow.

BISHOP: But I don't want to.

70

CARMEN: Shut up. Don't forget, in ten minutes in the State Room.
(ROSINE *re-enters*.)
ROSINE: Here I am again.
CARMEN: Here's your entire outfit, Sir. You're going to put it on.
Help him.
BISHOP: Go away! I need to be alone. Alice, my little Alice, tell her
that everything happened differently. . . .
ROSINE: Hold out your arms, Monsignor. You're going to wear the
lace alb.
BISHOP: But it's terrible. I shall be cold . . . I shall be hungry . . .
ROSINE: Touch the lace. Look, look . . . You're changing before
my very eyes. The Bishop is unfolding, unfurling, spreading
his wings . . . He's going to sing the *Kyrie Eleison*! Sing!
BISHOP: No!
ROSINE: Go on! Just one note.
BISHOP: I can't sing any more.
ROSINE: With me . . . very softly . . . very quietly . . . just the two
of us . . .
BISHOP: *Kyrie Eleison*.
ROSINE: *Christe Eleison*.
BISHOP: Are you there, Alice?
ROSINE: I'm here, Monsignor. I'm bringing you the mitre. Touch
it, Monsignor.
BISHOP: Leave me alone. *Please* . . .
ROSINE: Touch it . . . Give me your hand. Open your fingers . . .
now, just with the tips . . . touch it, that's all; remember how
pure you are – just touch it . . .
BISHOP: Don't . . . please . . . lace . . . vestments.
ROSINE: Good. Go on . . . vestments . . . go on . . . vestments.
BISHOP: Vestments, my beautiful garments, you protect me from
Life, from Earth, from Heaven. It is through you, it is to
enhance you, that I formulate my actions. From my actions,
which issue from you, from your tissue, issue my thoughts,
my words, and finally my message to the world. I am not
living, I am dancing . . .
ROSINE: Dance, little Bishop, dance . . . come along . . . dance.

A town square, in which patches of shadow predominate. In the background, some distance away, is the suggestion of the façade of the Grand Balcony, with closed shutters. CHANTAL *and* ROGER *are locked in each other's arms. Three men look as if they are watching them. Black suits. Black sweaters. They are holding machine pistols, and aiming them at the Grand Balcony.*

CHANTAL: This is the hour when the night breaks back before the day: let me go, my dove.

ROGER: Even a minute's separation from you will be unbearable.

CHANTAL: We won't be separated, I promise you. While I'm speaking to them in words of ice, I'll be speaking to you in whispers of love.

ROGER: They may keep you, Chantal. They're strong – strong as death.

CHANTAL: Don't be afraid, my love. Their strength has nothing like the power of your tenderness. I shall speak to them in a stern voice, I shall tell them the people's demands. And they'll listen to me because I am the revolution, its soul and its voice – and they'll be afraid. Let me go.

ROGER: (*With a cry*) Chantal! I love you!

CHANTAL: And I love you, because you are soft and sweet – you, the hardest and cruellest of men. And your softness and sweetness make you as light as a wisp of gauze, as subtle as a puff of mist, as airy as a whim. Your heavy muscles, your arms, your thighs and your hands are more unreal than the passing of day into night. You envelop me, and I contain you.

ROGER: Chantal, I love you, because you are hard and cruel – you, the softest and sweetest of women. Your softness and sweetness make you as cruel as a lesson, as hard as famine, as inflexible as ice. Your breasts, your skin and your hair are more real than the certainty of noon. You envelop me, and I contain you.

CHANTAL: When I'm with them – talking to them, I shall be listening inside myself to your sighs, and your groans, and to your heart beating. Let me go.

(*He holds her back.*)

ROGER: But I tore you – tore you from the grave! And now you're escaping, climbing, escaping *me*, ascending to the heavens. Your name's on the lips of people who have never seen or heard you. They think it's you they're fighting for. You're already a kind of saint. (*Furiously*) I didn't carry you off, steal you, for you to become a lion or a unicorn . . .

CHANTAL: Don't you like unicorns?

ROGER: I've never known how to make love to them – nor to you, either.

CHANTAL: You mean that I don't know how to love. I disappoint you.

ROGER: And I disappoint you. I can't communicate my love. I can't sing. In the end, it's always the song that counts.

LUKE: (*In a low voice*) It's time, Chantal. It's dawn.

CHANTAL: Listen – they're calling me.

ROGER: Let the others go.

CHANTAL: All they can do is fight, and all you can do is love. It's the role you've learnt to play. But I'm different. The brothel has taught me the art of acting many roles. I've played so many parts, I know them all. And I've had so many partners . . .

ROGER: Chantal!

CHANTAL: And such clever, such crafty, such eloquent ones, that my knowledge, my craft, my eloquence are incomparable. I can talk on equal terms with the Queen, the Hero, the Bishop, the Judge, the General, the Heroic Troops . . . and fool them all.

ROGER: And fool them all! You know everybody's part, don't you! Just now you weren't talking to me. You were just giving me my cues.

CHANTAL: They're not difficult to pick up.

LUKE: It's dawn!

ROGER: Chantal! Don't go!

CHANTAL: I'll come back; everything will be the same!

ROGER: Nothing will be the same. You'll be what you've always dreamed of being: an emblem, forever escaping from her appearance as a woman.

(CHANTAL *is led off by the revolutionaries*.)

The fight has left reality and entered the lists. Field Azure. The Combat of Allegories. Nobody, neither side, we none of us remember the reasons for our revolution any more.

*The balcony itself, projecting from the façade of the brothel. Facing the
audience are its closed shutters. Suddenly all the shutters open
automatically. The edge of the balcony reaches to the footlights. The*
BISHOP, *the* GENERAL *and the* JUDGE *are seen through the windows:
they are preparing themselves. Then both sides of the french window
open and they come out on to the balcony. First the* BISHOP, *then the*
GENERAL *and then the* JUDGE. *Finally, the* HERO. *And then the*
QUEEN: MADAM IRMA, *with a diadem on her forehead and wearing an
ermine cloak. All the characters come forward and take their places with
great diffidence. They don't speak. They are simply showing themselves.
They are all of exaggerated, gigantic proportions – except for the* HERO,
in other words, the CHIEF OF POLICE – *and dressed in their ceremonial
costumes which, however, are torn and dusty. Then, quite near them,
but not on the balcony, the* BEGGAR *appears.*

BEGGAR: (*In a sort of soft shout*) Long live the Queen.

  (*He goes out, as diffidently as he came. Finally, with the curtains
  blowing about in a strong wind,* CHANTAL *appears. The* QUEEN
  curtseys to her. There is a shot.* CHANTAL *falls. The* GENERAL
  and the QUEEN *carry away her dead body.*)

1ST PHOTOGRAPHER: (*To the* BISHOP) Look as if you're praying,
  will you, my Lord: the first thing is to drown the world in the
  image of a pious man.

BISHOP: (*Not moving*) In passionate meditation.

1ST PHOTOGRAPHER: Passionate. OK, get set.

BISHOP: (*Ill at ease*) Er . . . How?

1ST PHOTOGRAPHER: (*Laughing*) Don't you know how to look as if
  you're praying? All right, then: you face God and the camera
  at the same time. Hands together. Head up. Eyes down.
  That's the classic pose. Back to the status quo: back to
  classicism.

BISHOP: (*Kneeling*) Like this?

1ST PHOTOGRAPHER: (*Looking at him curiously*) Mm hm . . .
  (*Looking into his camera*) No, you're not in frame . . .

(*Still on his knees, the* BISHOP *moves into focus.*)
That's better.

2ND PHOTOGRAPHER: (*To the* JUDGE) Would you mind pulling a longer face, please? You don't look judge-like enough. A longer face . . .

JUDGE: Like a horse? Morose?

2ND PHOTOGRAPHER: Like a horse, *and* morose, my Lord. With both front feet on your documents . . . What I want is *the* judge. The good photographer produces the definitive image. The ar-che-type. Perfect.

1ST PHOTOGRAPHER: (*To the* BISHOP) Just a bit further round . . . (*He turns the* BISHOP's *head round.*)

BISHOP: (*Angrily*) The neck you're screwing off belongs to a prelate!

1ST PHOTOGRAPHER: My Lord Bishop – you should be praying in three-quarters profile.

2ND PHOTOGRAPHER: (*To the* JUDGE) My Lord Judge, if you can possibly manage it, just a bit more severity . . . if you could just drop your lower lip . . . (*Almost shouting*) That's it! Perfect! Don't move!
(*He runs back behind his camera, but before he can get there there is a flash: the* 1ST PHOTOGRAPHER *has got in first. The* 2ND *sticks his head under his black cloth.*)

GENERAL: (*To the* 3RD PHOTOGRAPHER) The best pose is Wellington's.

3RD PHOTOGRAPHER: (*Posing*) With the sword?

GENERAL: No no, that's Marlborough. No – with the arm outstretched, and the marshal's baton . . .

3RD PHOTOGRAPHER: Ah, you mean Napoleon?

GENERAL: I'm afraid I haven't got a baton . . .
(*In the mean time the* 1ST PHOTOGRAPHER *has gone over to the* BISHOP, *who hasn't moved, and is looking him up and down in silence.*)

3RD PHOTOGRAPHER: This'll do . . . Here you are – now take up your position.
(*He rolls up a sheet of paper to look like a marshal's baton, hands it to the* GENERAL, *who assumes his pose, then runs back to his camera. A flash: the* 2ND PHOTOGRAPHER *has got in first.*)

BISHOP: (*To the* 1ST PHOTOGRAPHER) I hope it'll come out well.

75

And now we ought to inundate the world with my image receiving the eucharist. Pity we haven't got a host knocking around anywhere . . .

1ST PHOTOGRAPHER: Leave it to us, my Lord. Journalists are ever-inventive. (*Calling*) My Lord! (*The* JUDGE *comes up*) I've got an idea for a great publicity stunt – give us your hand a minute, will you. (*Grabs him by the hand and moves him where he wants him.*) I only want your hand . . . That's it . . . Pull your sleeve up a bit . . . I want you to hold your hand over my Lord Bishop's tongue . . . (*Feels in his pocket. To the* BISHOP) Put your tongue out. More. That's it. (*Still feeling in his pockets. A flash. The* GENERAL *has just been photographed: he drops his pose.*) Bugger! I haven't got anything on me. (*Looking round him. To the* BISHOP) Don't move. May I?

(*Without waiting for an answer, he takes the* GENERAL'*s monocle out of his eye and goes back to the* BISHOP *and the* JUDGE. *He gets the* JUDGE *to hold the monocle over the* BISHOP'*s tongue, as if it were a host, and runs back to his camera. A flash.*

The QUEEN, *who has just come in with the* ENVOY, *has been watching them for some minutes.*)

QUEEN: But that's a false image – we won't have it!

ENVOY: It's a true image, born of a false spectacle.

1ST PHOTOGRAPHER: (*Derisively*) It's nothing new, your Majesty. When the rebels were being taken prisoner, we paid a policeman to kill a man in front of our cameras – actually he was just going to fetch me a packet of cigarettes. The photo showed a revolutionary shot while trying to escape.

QUEEN: Monstrous!

ENVOY: The Queen commands me to congratulate you, gentlemen. And she desires you to return to your posts.

(*The three* PHOTOGRAPHERS *put their heads under their black cloths. A silence.*)

QUEEN: (*Very softly, as if talking to herself*) Isn't he here?

ENVOY: (*Ironically, but elegantly*) If he is, he is invisible. He is occasionally to be encountered wandering, sombre and taciturn, in the corridors. He spends most of his time with specialists and tailors, trying on uniforms.

QUEEN: (*To the* ENVOY) You mustn't laugh at him. He has chosen a more difficult path towards illustriousness than ours.

(*Addressing the Three Great Figures, she reads from a paper she is holding*) We wish to thank you, gentlemen, for your devotion to our cause, to our people's cause, and for your noble conduct. Thanks to you and to the Chief of Police, the rebellion has been drowned in blood. There is nothing more to fear . . . (*Gives the paper back to the* ENVOY, *who keeps it in his hand.*) I hope.

BISHOP: Were it necessary to recommence the adventure, Madam, we are prepared. (*To the others*) Are we not, gentlemen? (*The others assent.*)

QUEEN: Thank you, thank you, gentlemen. (*With a benevolent, sad smile*) We notice it is you, my Lord Bishop, who are becoming the spokesman. No no, don't deny it. It is well that leadership should emanate from the highest spirituality. (*Pause.*) If only you hadn't had the abominable idea of having Chantal murdered . . .

BISHOP: (*Pretending to be frightened*) A stray bullet!

QUEEN: Who knows? Stray or not stray, Chantal was murdered on the Balcony – on my Balcony! When she'd simply come here to see me, to visit her boss.

BISHOP: I had the presence of mind to turn her into one of our saints . . . I had her image emblazoned on our flag.

QUEEN: It should have been *our* image . . .

BISHOP: You're already on the stamps, and the banknotes, and the rubber stamps in police stations. That's too much, as it is.

QUEEN: What! Too much?

ENVOY: Your Majesty must remain abstract *and* absent.

QUEEN: But I haven't even begun to get anything out of this adventure, yet. I like love, and I love power, and I want to experience them totally – with all of me.

ENVOY: (*Severely*) Then you should have joined the rebels. With them, if necessary, one could dominate through personal qualities. Our function is to found, to support and to justify metaphors.

QUEEN: Shall I never be who I am, then?

ENVOY: Never again.

QUEEN: (*As if alarmed*) Never again? Nothing will ever again relate just to me? Nothing that concerns me will ever be able to happen to other people?

ENVOY: (*Dryly*) No.

QUEEN: Every single event in my life: the way my blood pearls when I scratch myself . . .

ENVOY: Quite, Madam. Everything that concerns you will be written in capital letters.

QUEEN: But that's Death!

ENVOY: That is Death.

(*The* CHIEF OF POLICE *enters quietly, humbly.*)

CHIEF OF POLICE: (*Trying to smile*) I think . . . I think we've won . . . May I sit down? (*Sits down. Then he seems to be questioning them all with a look*) There's still nothing, I suppose?

ENVOY: (*Ironically*) Nothing. No one has yet felt the urge to destroy himself in your fascinating image.

CHIEF OF POLICE: Have you checked all the studios?

QUEEN: All of them, darling. If anything happens. I've given orders for all the bells to ring.

CHIEF OF POLICE: Any ideas? (*To the* PHOTOGRAPHERS) What about you?

1ST PHOTOGRAPHER: (*Showing him a photograph*) The executioner's red coat and his axe. I suggest amaranth red, and steel for the axe.

CHIEF OF POLICE: Already been done. Studio 14, otherwise known as the capital punishment studio. (*To the* 2ND PHOTOGRAPHER) And you, Sir?

2ND PHOTOGRAPHER: (*Showing his photograph*) I was reacting against a certain fashion that insists on brutality, and I preferred this romantic appearance . . .

(*The* CHIEF OF POLICE *makes an irritated gesture.*)

CHIEF OF POLICE: (*To the* 3RD PHOTOGRAPHER) And you, Sir? (*The* 3RD PHOTOGRAPHER *hands him a photograph.*) That's an exaggeration!

3RD PHOTOGRAPHER: But that's the image of yourself that haunts you, Sir, and it'll be certain to haunt them.

CHIEF OF POLICE: (*Angrily*) These masquerades, gentlemen, only show your lack of imagination. Maybe you're exhausted? Could Blood, Tears and even Sperm have lost their tragic, haughty power? (*He scrutinizes them*) Come to think of it, you do look a bit anaemic. No. I want my image to be both legendary *and* humane. People must be able to recognize my

face in it. Get back to your cameras. Go on!
(*The three* PHOTOGRAPHERS *go back under their black cloths.*)
Death and Glory still elude me. I've tried everything. I'm
wearing your sword, General.

GENERAL: Yes, I noticed. I hardly like to ask, but . . . er . . . could
I have it back?

CHIEF OF POLICE: (*Reproachfully*) General, how could you? My
Lord Judge, I have your executioner's whip, and your rosary,
my Lord Bishop. But still nothing, nothing, nothing,
nothing, nothing.

GENERAL: (*Plucking up courage*) You're going to find it very
difficult to achieve glory. All the seats have been reserved for a
long time. Every niche has its statue.

BISHOP: It's always the same when you start from scratch.

JUDGE: (*To the* CHIEF OF POLICE) You mustn't be impatient.
We've been waiting two thousand years to perfect our
roles . . .

GENERAL: (*Interrupting him*) Glory has to be won in battle. You
haven't sweated through enough glorious Waterloos. Get into
battle – or sit back and wait out the regulation two thousand
years.
(*Everyone laughs.*)

QUEEN: *We* are not amused.

CHIEF OF POLICE: (*Suddenly aroused*) The two thousand-year rule
must be waived. I demand glory. After all, I did save everything.

BISHOP: It was our age-old, tried and tested glory that upheld your
success.

CHIEF OF POLICE: A glory that I allow you.

BISHOP: Allow us? We have been chosen!

QUEEN: By whom?

BISHOP: (*Suddenly emphatic*) By Glory in person.

CHIEF OF POLICE: This masquerade?

BISHOP: It's within our power to change the meaning of this
masquerade. (*Authoritatively*) I am already the symbolic head
of the Church in this country, and I intend to become its actual
head. Instead of blessing and blessing and blessing *ad
nauseam*, I'm going to sign decrees, appoint priests, and build
a basilica. (*To the* JUDGE) How about you?

JUDGE: (*Looking at his wristwatch*) I shall make appointments,

79

draft new laws and revise the statute book. (*To the* GENERAL) And you?

GENERAL: Oh – all your ideas drift through my poor head like smoke through a log cabin. The art of war isn't as easy as all that.

BISHOP: (*Interrupting*) There's no difference. One's military fate can be read in the stars. Read your stars, for Christ's sake!

GENERAL: That's easy to say.

QUEEN: Watch it, George, watch it.

BISHOP: Somewhere in time, perhaps – in time or in space – there do exist high dignitaries endowed with absolute dignity, and dressed in genuine vestments.

QUEEN: (*Very angry*) Genuine! What about those, then?

BISHOP: Rabbit skin – sateen – machine-made lace – Do you think we're going to put up with a simulacrum for the rest of our lives?

CHIEF OF POLICE: Gentlemen, I don't quite follow you. You seem to be showing signs of wanting to act. It's true that at a decisive moment, at a time of certain conjunctures, I had to appeal to you in order to impose upon the rebellious people. I acknowledge the fact that you one and all rose magnificently to the situation but, gentlemen, your role was merely one of appearance, and I intend it to remain so.

BISHOP: You brought us together, because you wanted to consult us.

CHIEF OF POLICE: Not to consult you – to give you my orders.

GENERAL: You mean you don't want us to take part in your decisions?

CHIEF OF POLICE: In no way. It is I who command, I who organize everything. Be logical. If you are what you are, Judge, General or Bishop, it's because that was what you wanted to become, and what you wanted people to know you had become. Right?

GENERAL: More or less.

CHIEF OF POLICE: Good. So you have never done anything for its own sake: whatever you have done has always been a link in your becoming a Bishop, a Judge or a General.

BISHOP: That's both true and false. It's true in that every action *was* designed to lead us to the Glory we sought . . . It's false in that every action was charged with its own unique quality.

CHIEF OF POLICE: (*With a smile*) But that uniqueness was immediately nullified by each action always coming back to where it started from.

JUDGE: Which meant we achieved a greater dignity.

CHIEF OF POLICE: Exactly, my Lord, and it is precisely that dignity, become as inhuman as crystal, that renders you unfit to govern men.

BISHOP: You wouldn't be able to govern without the prestige that our dignity lends you.

CHIEF OF POLICE: Above you, and more sublime than you, is the Queen. It is from her that, for the moment, I derive my power and my rights. Above her is our standard, to which she must defer – our standard of Chantal Victorious, our saint.

BISHOP: Above her Majesty – whom we venerate – and above her flag, is God, who speaks through my voice.

CHIEF OF POLICE: And above God?

(*Silence.*)

Well, gentlemen, have you no answer? Above God – *you* – without whom God would be as nothing. And above you – *me* – without whom you would be as nothing.

JUDGE: What about the people?

CHIEF OF POLICE: They're on their knees before God!

(*All four burst out laughing.*)

BISHOP: (*Very pedantically*) This is where the question – a very serious question – arises: are you going to use what we represent to serve you, or are we going to use you to serve what we represent?

CHIEF OF POLICE: (*Angrily*) I have intelligence and strength on my side.

BISHOP: So *you* can be argued with. Our power is obscure, and therefore indisputable.

CHIEF OF POLICE: (*Standing up*) Chatty, aren't you!

BISHOP: (*Standing up*) Shout more loudly than I if you wish, but do not forget my dignity.

CHIEF OF POLICE: Pah! It was I who nominated you. It was I who dug you out of a room in a brothel . . .

BISHOP: (*Furious*) Exactly. So long as we were in a room in a brothel we belonged to our own fantasies. But since we've exposed them, given them a name and made them public, there has been a bond between us and other men, between us and you, and now we've no alternative but to carry on with this adventure according to the laws of visibility.

CHIEF OF POLICE: You have absolutely no power.

BISHOP: But you want us to have some over the people. For us to have power over them, you must first recognize that we have some over you.

CHIEF OF POLICE: ⎱
QUEEN: ⎰ Never!

BISHOP: (*Standing*) Right. Then we'll go back to our rooms and continue our search for an absolute dignity. We ought never to have left them. We were perfectly happy there until you came and dug us out. We were in a state of grace, Sir. We were absolutely safe. It was peaceful and pleasant behind the shutters and padded curtains, we were protected by attentive women, we were protected by a police force that protects brothels, we could be General, Judge and Bishop until we reached perfection – and paroxysm! You dragged us brutally out of that marvellous, enviable, blessed state.

GENERAL: (*Interrupting the* BISHOP) My breeches! What a joy it is to pull on my breeches! I shall sleep with my general's breeches on, I shall live in my general's breeches. I'm a general like other people are bishops.

JUDGE: I am simply a dignity represented by petticoats.

GENERAL: (*To the* BISHOP) There is no one moment when I start preparing myself! In the old days, it was a month in advance! – preparing myself to put on my general's breeches or boots. Now, I wear them for all eternity. My goodness! I'm not dreaming any more.

BISHOP: You see, he isn't dreaming any more. Our vestimental purity, our luxurious, sterile – and sublime – appearance has been eroded. It will never return: so be it. But we have had the bitter-sweet taste of action and responsibility: that taste remains with us and we find it agreeable. Our rooms are no longer secret. You hurt us when you dragged us out into the light, but we are going to live in the light, with all that that implies. Judge, Bishop and General, from now on all our actions will lead to the progressive reduction in importance of those vestments and dignities: we are going to put them to use. But if you want them to be of use, and of use to you – since it is your order that we have chosen to defend, then you must be the first to recognize and respect them.

QUEEN: George! Pull yourself together. *Please*! They'll devour us!

CHIEF OF POLICE: I'm so weak, so awkward . . .

BISHOP: You can see how his failure is preying on him. Our power . . .

QUEEN: George! Hey! Defend yourself! It was God Himself who chose us . . .

ENVOY: (*Admiringly*) Sublime! Continue . . .

QUEEN: (*To the* CHIEF OF POLICE) Come on! God helps those who help themselves! Rise above yourself . . .! Real blood is flowing in my veins, there's real sweat under my armpits, I'm on fire – and I want power!

CHIEF OF POLICE: You have spoken admirably. I must compliment you on your eloquence, your elocution, the limpidity of your timbre and the power of your organ. I'm only a man of action, and I get a bit tangled up with words and ideas when they have no immediate application. Which is why for the last few seconds I've been wondering whether to send you back to your niches, like dogs to their kennels . . .

GENERAL: Now look here!

(*The* CHIEF OF POLICE *gives the* GENERAL *a push. The* GENERAL *goes flying and ends up, flabbergasted, on the floor*.)

CHIEF OF POLICE: (*As if talking to a dog*) Down, Sir! Lie down, General! You're stuck, and it's not me that's stopping you functioning, it's the skirts of your dignities.

JUDGE: I can tuck mine up . . .

(*The* CHIEF OF POLICE *gives the* JUDGE *a push. The* JUDGE *goes flying*.)

CHIEF OF POLICE: Down, Sir! Seeing that you want to be recognized as a judge, would you still want to be recognized, according to my idea of what a judge is? And according to the general idea of your dignities? Right. Then I shall have to move further towards that sort of recognition, shan't I? Shall I or shan't I?

(*No one answers*.)

Well? Shall I or shan't I?

(*The* BISHOP *prudently moves away*.)

JUDGE: (*Timidly, picking himself up*) We could try – cautiously of course – to incline in a slightly different direction . . .

GENERAL: Are you mad? If we start thinking, people might follow our thoughts, and where would it all end?

CHIEF OF POLICE: Well said, General. And after all, when all's said and done – you are still in the brothel!

QUEEN: (*Moved*) My hero speaks so well!

(*One after the other, the three men sigh deeply*.)

CHIEF OF POLICE: That's a comfort to you, isn't it? You never really wanted to get outside yourselves, did you?

(*They shake their heads*.)

I understand. (*Amicably*) Me too, you know – it even happens to me: when I'm too tired after I've been inventing things for men, when I'm too harassed by the weight of my power and responsibility – even *I* feel like escaping into an image of myself. But my image, alas, is still in the making. As you know, it still doesn't feature in the brothel nomenclature.

QUEEN: The pink book.

CHIEF OF POLICE: The pink book. (*Suddenly very weary*) Come, gentlemen, I'm a poor creature, won't you take pity on me? (*He looks at them one by one*.) Oh come, gentlemen, – how can you be so hard hearted?

(*The three men hang their heads*.)

You are silent. What more must I say? Don't you see that in my desire to shoulder all the responsibility for every action there is a certain affection for you? And a great deal of generosity? (*Very sadly*) And you, instead of being grateful to me and helping me by an ever greater passivity – you are determined to give up your admirable, comfortable finery. Yet it was for you that, little by exquisite little, these illustrious rites were perfected. All that work, all that patience, over all those centuries! You have a chance to benefit from all this, and you want to go back up into the light of day?

GENERAL: But what about you . . .?

CHIEF OF POLICE: It's harder for me. I have to try and bring into being a new type, a new illustration. But oh, the trials and tribulations! And shall I ever ever succeed?

BISHOP: We all hope so. (*Looking at the others*) Don't we, gentlemen?

JUDGE: ⎫
GENERAL: ⎬ Yes, we really do hope so.

CHIEF OF POLICE: (*Very moved*) Thank you. Thank you, my
friends.

(*A fairly long silence, during which the* CHIEF OF POLICE *seems
to be wiping away tears.*)

JUDGE: People do fear you, though. People dread you, and envy
you.

CHIEF OF POLICE: I'm afraid that people fear, or envy, a man, but
not . . . (*Searching for his words*) . . . not a wrinkle, for
instance, or a curl . . . or a cigar . . . You know – something
individual.

GENERAL: Haven't there been any suggestions?

CHIEF OF POLICE: Oh, lots. The last was suggested only a
moment ago – but really, I hardly dare mention it.

JUDGE: You mean you've decided against it?

CHIEF OF POLICE: Yes . . . practically . . . no . . . I don't know . . .
that is, if I really had to . . .

GENERAL: Was it . . . very audacious?

CHIEF OF POLICE: Very. Extremely. I'd never dare tell you.

BISHOP: Even in confession?

JUDGE: In confession, you'd be the only one to know. What about
us?

BISHOP: (*Severely*) I'm only trying to liberate an unhappy
conscience.

CHIEF OF POLICE: Gentlemen – I can rely on your judgement and
loyalty. This is a battle of ideas, after all. Anyway, I don't
know which way to turn. The last suggestion was . . . was . . .
well . . . was that I should appear as a giant phallus – a
man-sized prick.

(*The three men look thunderstruck.*)

QUEEN: George! You?

CHIEF OF POLICE: Well, if I'm to symbolize the nation . . .

QUEEN: George!

ENVOY: Take no notice, Ma'am. They all talk like that, these days.

JUDGE: A phallus? And man-sized? You mean: enormous?

CHIEF OF POLICE: My size.

JUDGE: But that would be very difficult to bring off.

CHIEF OF POLICE: Not so specially. With all their new

85

techniques, our rubber goods industry is quite capable of perfecting some very interesting objects. No, that isn't what's worrying me, it's rather . . . (*Turning to the* BISHOP) . . . what the Church would think of it?

BISHOP: (*After some reflection*) No definite pronouncement can be made this evening. The idea is indeed audacious, but if it seemed that you were in desperate straits we might perhaps consider the question. It would, in fact, be a formidable disguise, and if you were to go down to posterity in that form, from generation to generation . . . (*He makes a vague gesture.*)

CHIEF OF POLICE: Do you advise against it?

GENERAL: (*Timidly*) Perhaps if we painted it in our national colours?

JUDGE: And inscribed a legal text on it?

BISHOP: If we released the dove of the Holy Spirit from it?

GENERAL: (*Forcefully*) It must become a patriotic emblem.

JUDGE: It will serve the magistracy. The rod of justice . . .

BISHOP: (*Authoritatively*) It will bear witness to the most venerable principle in the world, though it be laboured with scratches, whipped, worn with furrows and wounds . . .

GENERAL: (*Forcefully*) It will be the flagstaff!

JUDGE: The scourge!

BISHOP: (*Summing up*) The reason for our hatred!

QUEEN: But we haven't got room for it, we haven't equipped a studio . . .

CHIEF OF POLICE: (*Gently*) Would you like to see the model?

ALL: (*Shocked*) No!

CHIEF OF POLICE: (*Calming them with a gesture*) Anyway, I'm not sure I like it, yet. (*Suddenly violent*) But I refuse to consider myself beaten! (*Almost humbly, and suddenly looking very tired*) Wait a little longer. One day something will happen, and I shall be able to stop being so hard. I'll worm my way into people's minds – and rot.

(*Enter* CARMEN, *almost furtively, by the door on the left. The* ENVOY *is the first to see her, and he silently indicates her presence to the* QUEEN. *The* QUEEN *signs to her to go away, but* CARMEN *nevertheless takes a step forward.*)

QUEEN: (*Almost whispering*) I gave orders we weren't to be disturbed. What do you want? (CARMEN *is still walking towards her.*)

86

CARMEN: I want a word with you.

QUEEN: All right, then: what is it?

CARMEN: (*Hesitating*) It's . . . I don't know . . .

QUEEN: (*Resigned*) Come on: when at Court, do as the Court does, and let's keep our voices down.

(*She is listening rather obviously to* CARMEN *who leans over and murmurs a few words. The* QUEEN *looks very upset.*)

Are you sure?

CARMEN: Yes, Madam.

(*The* QUEEN *suddenly hurries out, left, followed by* CARMEN. *The* CHIEF OF POLICE *starts to follow them, but the* ENVOY *stops him.*)

ENVOY: Her Majesty may not be followed.

CHIEF OF POLICE: But what's happening? Where's she going?

ENVOY: (*Ironically*) To her embroidery. The Queen is embroidering, and she is not embroidering . . .

CHIEF OF POLICE: Oh, not again!

ENVOY: The Queen attains her reality when she withdraws, absents herself, or dies.

GENERAL: You don't think, perhaps, that . . .?

CHIEF OF POLICE: (*Almost trembling*) You mean . . .?

BISHOP: Yes. After all, the people have lost all hope.

GENERAL: And if they've lost all hope, they've lost everything.

JUDGE: And if they've lost everything, they might come here and lose themselves . . .

CHIEF OF POLICE: In me!

BISHOP: Why not?

CHIEF OF POLICE: In short, I'll be like a pond where they can come and look at their reflections?

GENERAL: (*Delighted, and bursting out laughing*) And if they lean over a little too far, they'll fall in and drown. Any minute now you'll be full of drowned bodies! (*No one seems to share his amusement.*) Well . . . they haven't even got to the edge of the pond, yet. (*Embarrassed*) We'll have to wait.

(*A silence.*)

(*The door, left, suddenly opens, and the* QUEEN *appears, looking radiant.*)

QUEEN: George! (*She falls into the* CHIEF OF POLICE'*s arms.*)

CHIEF OF POLICE: (*Incredulous*) It's not true! (*The* QUEEN *nods.*)

But where? . . . When? . . .

QUEEN: (*Showing great emotion*) There! . . . Now . . .

CHIEF OF POLICE: You're having me on: I didn't hear anything.
You said there'd be bells.

(*There is a sudden tremendous ringing of bells – a sort of carillon.*)

QUEEN: He's coming. Quick! Quick!

(*They all take up watching positions.*)

SCENE 13

Description of the Mausoleum:

*Something like the interior of a tower, or of a well. The wall is
circular; its stones are visible. At the rear, a staircase leading
downwards. In the centre of the well there seems to be another well, with
the first few steps of another staircase. Four laurel wreaths, decorated
with black crêpe, adorn the walls. When the two sides of the mirror have
separated,* ROGER *is in the middle of the staircase, walking down it.*
CARMEN *seems to be guiding him.* ROGER *is dressed like the*
CHIEF OF POLICE, *but as he is wearing the same buskins as the three
figureheads, he looks taller. His shoulders have been broadened, too. He
walks down the stairs to the rhythm of a drum.*

CARMEN: (*Going up to him and handing him a cigar*) With the
compliments of the house.

ROGER: (*Putting the cigar into his mouth*) Thank you.

CARMEN: (*Taking it out again*) That end's – for the light. This end's
– for your mouth. (*She turns the cigar round.*) Is this your first
cigar?

ROGER: Yes . . . (*A pause.*) Anyway, I don't need your advice.
You're here to serve. I've paid . . .

CARMEN: I beg your pardon, Sir.

ROGER: Where's the slave?

CARMEN: They're just untying him.

ROGER: Does he know what it's all about?

CARMEN: He knows everything. You know you're the first, you're
inaugurating this studio. Mind you, all the scripts can be
reduced to one major theme . . .

ROGER: Which is?

CARMEN: Death.

ROGER: (*Looking about*) So this is my tomb?

CARMEN: (*Correcting him*) Mausoleum.

ROGER: How many slaves are working on it?

CARMEN: The entire population, Sir. Half on night shift and half on day shift. In accordance with your wishes, the whole mountain is going to be excavated. The interior will be as complex as an ant's nest, or the Basilica at Lourdes, we don't know which, yet. Nobody will be able to see anything from outside. All they'll know is that it's a sacred mountain, but inside tombs are already being entombed in tombs, cenotaphs in cenotaphs, coffins in coffins, urns . . .

ROGER: And where am I now?

CARMEN: (*With a gesture that disclaims responsibility*) In an antechamber. An antechamber called the Valley de los Caídos. You'll be going further down, soon.

ROGER: I mustn't hope to see the light of day ever again.

CARMEN: (*Perplexed*) Do you still want to?

(*A silence.*)

ROGER: Is it really true that no one has ever been here before me?

CARMEN: In this . . . tomb, or in this . . . studio?

(*A silence.*)

ROGER: Is everything exactly right? My costume? My toupee?

CHIEF OF POLICE: He knows I wear a toupee?

BISHOP: (*With a mocking laugh, to the* JUDGE *and the* GENERAL) Everyone knows.

CARMEN: (*To* ROGER) We've been working on this for a long time. Everything is exactly as it should be. The rest is up to you.

ROGER: (*Worried*) I'm feeling my way too, you know. I have to decide what I think the Hero's like – he's never shown himself much.

CARMEN: That's why we brought you to the Mausoleum Studio. Not too many mistakes possible – nor fantasies.

(*A pause.*)

ROGER: Shall I be alone?

CARMEN: Everything's padded. The doors, the walls . . .

ROGER: (*Hesitantly*) And . . . the Mausoleum itself?

CARMEN: Carved in the rock.

ROGER: Prove it!

CARMEN: There's water seeping through the wall.

ROGER: The silence?

CARMEN: Deathly.

ROGER: The night?

CARMEN: A darkness so dense that your eyes have developed incomparable qualities.

ROGER: The cold?

CARMEN: Of death. A gigantic effort has violated the mountain. Men are still groaning as they carve out your granite niche. All of which goes to show that the people love you, and that you're a conqueror.

ROGER: Groaning? Could I . . . Could I hear them groaning?

(*She turns to a hole at the foot of the wall from which the* BEGGAR's *head emerges. He's the* SLAVE *now.*)

CARMEN: Come here!

(*The* SLAVE *comes crawling in.*)

ROGER: (*Looking the* SLAVE *up and down*) Is that it?

CARMEN: Gorgeous, isn't he. Starved, covered with lice and sores. He dreams of dying for you. Shall I leave you, now?

ROGER: With him? Oh no. (*A pause.*) Don't go. Everything always happens in the presence of a woman. It's to have a woman's face as witness that people usually . . .

(*The sound of a hammer hitting an anvil is suddenly heard, and then a cock crowing.*)

Is life so close?

CARMEN: (*In a normal voice, not acting*) I told you: everything's padded, but some sounds always manage to filter through. Does it worry you? Little by little life is starting up again . . . as before . . .

ROGER: (*Looking uneasy*) Yes, as before . . .

CARMEN: (*Gently*) Were you?

ROGER: (*Very sadly*) Yes. It's all fucked . . . the saddest thing of all is when people say: 'The revolution was so wonderful!'

CARMEN: You mustn't think about it any more. And you must stop listening to the sounds of the outside world. Anyway, it's raining. A tornado has been raging over the mountain. (*In a stage voice*) Make yourself at home here. (*Pointing to the* SLAVE) Get him to talk.

ROGER: (*Playing his part: to the* SLAVE) So you can talk, can you? What else can you do?

SLAVE: (*Lying flat on his stomach*) To begin with, I can grovel, and after that I can shrink even more. (*He takes hold of* ROGER's *foot and puts it on his own back*.) Like this! . . . and even –

ROGER: (*Impatiently*) Yes . . . and even . . .?

SLAVE: Sink into the earth, if that's possible.

ROGER: (*Puffing at his cigar*) Sink into the earth – really? But there isn't any mud.

QUEEN: (*Speaking off*) He's right. We should have thought of the mud. In a well-run house . . . Still it is the first day, and he's christening the Studio . . .

SLAVE: (*To* ROGER) I can feel it all round my body, Sir. It's all over me, except in my mouth – which I keep open so as to sing your praises, and emit the groans that have made me famous.

ROGER: Famous? Are you famous? You?

SLAVE: Famous for my songs, Sir, which hymn your glory.

ROGER: Then your glory goes hand in hand with mine. (*To* CARMEN) Does he mean that my reputation will depend on his words? And that . . . if he stops singing, I shan't exist any more . . .?

CARMEN: (*Dryly*) I'd like to help you, but you keep asking questions that aren't in the script.

ROGER: (*To the* SLAVE) And you – who hymns you?

SLAVE: No one. I'm dying.

ROGER: But without me, without my blood, sweat and tears, what would you be?

SLAVE: Nothing.

ROGER: (*To the* SLAVE) So you sing. What else do you do?

SLAVE: We do our utmost to be increasingly unworthy of you.

ROGER: Such as?

SLAVE: To stand still and rot. It isn't always easy, believe me. Life tries to get the better of us . . . But we resist. We dwindle a bit more every –

ROGER: Day?

SLAVE: Week.

CHIEF OF POLICE: (*Speaking off*) That's not much. With a bit of effort . . .

ENVOY: (*To the* CHIEF OF POLICE) Hush. Let them play their parts through to the end . . .

ROGER: That's not much. With a bit of effort . . .

SLAVE: (*Exalted*) I should be overjoyed, your Excellency. You are so beautiful. So beautiful, that I wonder whether you are all radiance, or all the shadows of all the nights.

ROGER: What does it matter, when from now on my only reality will be that of your words?

SLAVE: (*Dragging himself*) You have no mouth, no eyes, no ears, and yet you're all thundering mouth and dazzling, watchful eye.

ROGER: *You* can see all that, *you*, but the others, can they see? Does the night know? Does death? Do the stones? Yes, the stones – what do the stones say?

SLAVE: (*Still dragging himself along on his belly*) The stones say . . .

ROGER: Go on: I'm listening.

SLAVE: (*Stops crawling, and turns to face the audience*) The cement that binds us all together to make your tomb . . .

CHIEF OF POLICE: (*Turning to face the audience and beating his breast with joy*) Even the stones have heard of me!

SLAVE: (*Continuing*) . . . the cement is moulded with tears, spit and blood. Resting their hands and eyes on us the masons mould us from their grief. We are yours – and only yours.
(*The* SLAVE *continues his crawl*.)

ROGER: (*Becoming increasingly exalted*) Everything speaks of me! Everything breathes me, everything adores me! My life has been lived so that a glorious page might be written, and then read. It's the reading that counts.
(*He suddenly notices that the* SLAVE *has disappeared, and says to* CARMEN:)
But . . . where's he going? . . . Where is he?

CARMEN: Gone to sing. He's returning to the light of day. He'll say . . . that he wears your footprints . . . and that . . .

ROGER: (*Anxiously*) Yes, and that . . .? What else will he say?

CARMEN: The truth: that you are dead, or rather, that you never stop dying, and that your image, like your name, is reverberating to infinity.

ROGER: He knows that my image is everywhere?

CARMEN: Everywhere. Inscribed. Engraved. Enforced by fear.

ROGER: In the palms of dockers? In the games of children? On the teeth of soldiers? In war?

CARMEN: Everywhere.

CHIEF OF POLICE: (*Speaking off*) I've arrived, then?

QUEEN: (*Touched*) Are you happy?

CHIEF OF POLICE: You've done well. The finishing touch to your house.

ROGER: (*To* CARMEN) Is it in prisons, my image, in the wrinkles of old men?

CARMEN: Yes.

ROGER: In the bends of roads?

CARMEN: You mustn't ask the impossible.

(*The same sounds as before: the cock and the anvil.*)

CARMEN: Your time's up, Sir. That's the end of the session. You go out to the left. The corridor . . .

(*The sound of the anvil again, a little more loudly.*)

Do you hear? You must go . . . What are you doing?

ROGER: Life is very near . . . and very far. All the women here are beautiful . . . That's all they are for. You can lose yourself in them . . .

CARMEN: (*Harshly*) Yes. In everyday language we're called tarts. But you must go . . .

ROGER: Go where? Back into life? And take up where I left off, as they say . . .?

CARMEN: (*Slightly anxiously*) I don't know what you do for a living, and I'm not allowed to ask. But you've got to go. Your time's up.

(*The sound of the anvil, and other noises that represent some sort of activity: the crack of a whip, the sound of an engine, etc.*)

ROGER: They're in a hell of a hurry in your house. Why d'you want me to go back where I came from?

CARMEN: There's nothing more for you to do . . .

ROGER: There? No. Nothing at all. Nor here, either. And out there, in what you call life, everything has been destroyed. Truth wasn't possible . . . Did you know Chantal?

CARMEN: (*Suddenly terrified*) You must go! Hurry up and go!

QUEEN: (*Irritated*) I won't have him disturbing the peace in my studios. Who sent me that bastard? It's always the same: after the troubles, you get the villains. I hope Carmen . . .

CARMEN: (*To* ROGER) Get out! You aren't allowed to ask me questions, either. You must know that brothels are very strictly regulated, and that we're protected by the police. Get out!

93

ROGER: No! Seeing that I'm playing the part of the Chief of Police, and that I'm authorized to be here.

CARMEN: (*Tugging at him*) You're mad! There's always someone who imagines he's suddenly come to power . . . Come on! Get out!

ROGER: (*Freeing himself*) If the brothel exists, and if I have the right to come here, then I have an equal right to take my chosen character to the limit of its destiny . . . no, of mine . . . to merge his destiny with mine . . .

CARMEN: Don't shout so, Sir: all the studios are occupied. Come on . . .

ROGER: Nothing! I've got nothing left! But the Hero won't have much left, either . . .

(CARMEN *tries to get him out. She opens one door, then another, and then another . . . none is the right one . . .* ROGER *has pulled out a knife and, with his back to the audience, makes the gesture of castrating himself.*)

QUEEN: On my rugs! On my carpet! He's a maniac!

CARMEN: (*Shrieking*) Doing that here! . . . (*Calling out*) Madam! Madam Irma . . . !

(CARMEN *finally manages to drag* ROGER *out.*
The QUEEN *runs out of the room.*)

SCENE 14

CHIEF OF POLICE: (*Moving to the centre of the stage*) Well played. Well played! Thought he'd got me for a moment. (*His hands go to his flies. Very obviously he feels the weight of his balls, then reassured, heaves a sigh of relief.*) Still there – thank God! Still intact, gentlemen, still intact! My image may not be, but I am. The plumber just didn't understand his role – that's all.

ENVOY: Well done, Chief.

CHIEF OF POLICE: Did you see? Did you see me? There? Just now? Larger than large, stronger than strong, deader than dead? Did you see. Irma, Irma, it's happened! I've arrived! My image! I belong to the nomenclature. I've got my simulacrum! Goal!

(*The* BISHOP, *the* JUDGE, *the* GENERAL, *the* ENVOY *congratulate the* CHIEF OF POLICE.)

CHIEF OF POLICE: Irma – I've done it, Irma, I've done it. (*The* CHIEF OF POLICE *weeps tears of happiness.*)
    (*Enter* IRMA, *followed by the entire cast, including* ARTHUR, CHANTAL *and* ROGER – *they are smiling broadly – they all slap him on the back, shake hands, etc.*)
CHIEF OF POLICE: I invite you all to glorify me. To glorify my functions.
    (*Organ music is heard.*) Let us pray.
ALL: Our father which art in Heaven . . .
    (*They start building the tomb, praying and singing the while.*)
CHIEF OF POLICE: (*In a low, ardent voice*) My drama is beginning to be played. A living image of me will be perpetuated in secret for ever and ever. From this moment on – everything is changed . . .
QUEEN: George, I still love you!
CHIEF OF POLICE: I've earned the right to sit and wait for two thousand years! Irma, tell them to send up enough grub for two thousand years! (*He starts backing into his tomb.*)
QUEEN: What about me, George! I'm still alive!
CHIEF OF POLICE: Masses will be said to my glory. Low Masses. For posterity – shoot! (*Three practically simultaneous flashes.*) And now I shall be able to be good! And godly! And just!
QUEEN: George!
CHIEF OF POLICE: I've won!
QUEEN: Don't go, George – wait!
CHIEF OF POLICE: Remember me!
ALL: (*As they finish walling him up*) Amen!
IRMA: (*Starting to undress*) Gentlemen, you are free!
BISHOP: In the middle of the night?
IRMA: You can go by the little door that opens on to the alleyway. There's a car.
    (*The cast start to exit.*
    A burst of machine-gun fire.)
IRMA: What's that? Our side . . . or the rebels . . . or what?
ENVOY: Someone dreaming, Ma'am. (CARMEN *exits.*)
IRMA: Irma, call me Irma, and go home. Goodnight.
ENVOY: Goodnight, Madam Irma. (*Exits*).
IRMA: (*Alone, switching off lights*) What a lot of lights . . . More bills! Thirty-eight studios . . . Every one gilded, every one

capable of combining with the others, somehow . . . And all these performances, just for me to be left alone, mistress and assistant mistress of this house and of myself . . . (*She turns off another light, and then changes her mind.*) Ah no, that's the tomb, he's going to want light for the next two thousand years! . . . And food . . . (*Shrugs her shoulders*) Glory consists of descending to the grave with tons of grub! (*Turns towards the wings, and calls*) Carmen? . . . Carmen? . . . (*Goes on switching off lights.*) Any minute now we'll have to start all over again . . . put all the lights on . . . get dressed . . . (*A cock crows.*) . . . get dressed . . . oh, all these disguises! Cast all the parts again . . . play mine . . . (*Stops in the centre of the stage, facing the audience*) . . . prepare yours . . . judges, generals, bishops, chamberlains, revolutionaries who let the revolution congeal . . . I'm going to prepare my costumes and my studios for tomorrow . . . You must go home, now – and you can be quite sure that nothing there will be any more real than it is here . . . You must go . . . You go out on the right, down the alleyway . . . It's morning . . . (*Puts out the last light.*)

(*A burst of machine-gun fire.*)